foreword

Thailand has a well-earned reputation as being the Land of a Thousand Smiles, not least because of its warm and friendly people who greet everyone with a *wai*—the palms placed together with a gentle bow of the head. *Mai pen rai*, which means "it doesn't matter", is a commonly-heard expression everywhere in Thailand. This relaxed attitude is what visitors to Thailand have come to love, along with all the country's charms—from its ancient temples and tantalising cuisine to pristine beaches and virgin tropical rainforests. Some might say that Thailand seems almost designed to delight the senses.

To reflect this uniquely Thai state of mind, the Tourism Authority of Thailand (TAT) recently launched its new tourism promotion campaign, Thailand...Happiness on Earth. We hope more people worldwide will be encouraged to come and experience Thai-style happiness for themselves.

From elephant camps to world-class beach resorts, Thailand has something to offer every kind of traveller. Colourful festivals, majestic heritage sights, botanically blessed resorts, excellent shopping experiences and blissful spas are all part of the treasures Thailand has to offer the world. Whatever your plans, the warm Thai hospitality will make any holiday here unforgettable.

All year long, the tropical weather makes Thailand ideal for vacations in the sun, whether in the cities and towns, or beside sapphire beaches and age-old rivers synonymous with the Thai way of life. Getting around is a cinch with Thailand's modern transport network that links the islands and towns with major international airports or train stations. With the unique combination of timeless and contemporary, and rich culture combined with natural wonders, Thailand offers many delightful ways to discover happiness on earth.

Juthamas Siriwan
Governor, Tourism Authority of Thailand

THIS PAGE (FROM TOP): *Revered in Buddhism, the delicate lotus dwarfs a tiny frog; Royal Grand Palace.*

THAILAND...HAPPINESS ON EARTH

It has been said that happiness is a state of mind. It is indeed ethereal, a feel-good emotion that captures the senses. Yet there is one destination where happiness is embodied everywhere you turn: The Kingdom of Thailand. With its blend of East and West, ancient and modern, Thailand exudes Happiness on Earth. All year round, its charms beckon with the promise of joy in all its forms.

gracious happiness

The easy-going and gracious nature of the Thai people has earned the country its moniker as the Land of Smiles. Hospitality comes naturally to the Thais, an outstanding characteristic that places them on top of the list any time people talk about excellent service. The Thais certainly know how to live life and enjoy it graciously. Whether working in the air-conditioned comforts of a city office or under the sweltering heat of the midday sun, they are always blessed with a ready smile and an eagerness to show visitors to Thailand why their country is one of the happiest places on earth.

majestic happiness

UNESCO has recognised a number of World Heritage Sites in Thailand and the Thais take much pride in preserving this rich, majestic past. Visitors can share in this delight by visiting the Sukhothai Historical Park, first capital of the Siamese Kingdom, and Old Siam's second capital city, Ayutthaya, now the Ayutthaya Historical Park. Besides these man-made marvels, Thailand also boasts breathtaking natural wonders, such as Thung Yai Naresuan—Huai Kha Kaeng National Park. The largest forest conservation area in Southeast Asia protected by law, the Park is home to birds and animals that have become extinct in other parts of the world. Yet here in Thailand, they thrive in happiness.

THIS PAGE (FROM TOP): With glorious colours, it is no wonder Thailand is the Land of Smiles; cycling holidays take on new levels of adventure and wonder.

OPPOSITE (FROM TOP): Thailand regularly organises scintillating festivals such as Loi Krathong (Festival of Lights); white sand and blue seas leave you wanting for nothing more.

festive happiness

A holiday in Thailand wouldn't be complete without experiencing one of its many festivals and special events. Besides traditional celebrations like Songkran (Thai New Year) and Loi Krathong (Festival of Light), Thailand also plays hosts to international events like the Bangkok International Film Festival and the Pattaya International Music Festival throughout the year.

One perennial favourite is the Thailand Grand Sale, which starts in June and lasts for two months. It's bargains galore throughout the sale period as shopaholics enjoy discounts and promotions at department stores, restaurants, hotels and other retail outlets throughout the country.

The festive atmosphere carries through to the everyday with Thai food—one of the greatest cuisines in the world—available everywhere from roadside stalls to five-star restaurants. Indeed, in Thailand, every day is a celebration.

relaxing happiness

Thailand's beautiful rivers and canals not only serve as important transportation routes, but also provide the essentials for life. The picture of everyday living on the waters is often breathtakingly scenic—old rice barges laden with goods, fishermen working from romantic long tail boats, and merchants selling fresh produce in floating markets. Much as they were centuries ago, Thai waterways are still major arteries of trade, commerce and leisure. Ferries, barges, water-taxis and all manner of large and small water craft form an unforgettable panorama for the visitor.

Thailand's famous beaches and tropical islands are also the perfect hideaways for guests seeking the ultimate in rest and relaxation. Powdery white sand, clear turquoise water and an abundance of marine life make Thailand's beaches some of the best in the world. Whether diving amongst tropical fish, wandering along the sea shore with a companion, or simply lazing under a palm tree, listening to the lapping waves, a holiday in Thailand is perfect for those needing to unwind.

blissful happiness

The art of traditional Thai healing dates back hundred of years, yet it is only recently that the world has discovered the benefits of these age-old practices. The most famous of these is the Thai massage, where the stretching and manipulation of aching muscles and pressure points restore balance among the body's elements. Intrepid visitors can not only experience this sublime experience, but—if they are so inclined—also learn the techniques and intricacies of this ancient therapeutic art. Additionally, Thailand has earned a reputation in recent years for offering some of the best health and beauty spas in the world. Some of these have become destinations unto themselves, where guests can indulge in a range of beauty and body treatments to heal, rebalance and restore the senses.

convenient happiness

With its extensive transport network, getting around Thailand is wonderfully easy. By road, rail, air, or across water, Thailand's transportation infrastructure is constantly expanding to cater to the demands of travellers eager to reach the farthest corners of the country. Of course, shorter distances are easily covered by metered taxis, buses or the iconic tuk tuks that zip about easily even in the busiest traffic conditions. In Bangkok, the elevated BTS Skytrain boasts two routes running north and east of the city.

This is in addition to its mass transit subway system that stretches over 20 km (12 miles) under the metropolis, linking hotels with shopping and entertainment areas, conference centres and tourist attractions. The opening of Bangkok's new international Suvarnabhumi Airport promises improved departure and arrival procedures, as well as easy access to your next port of call.

THIS PAGE (FROM TOP): Luxury spas all over the country pamper their visitors with traditional Thai treatments and massages; modern Bangkok trains are very convenient for visitors.

OPPOSITE: Romantic yet practical, bright umbrellas provide shade from the dazzling sun.

With its extensive transport network, getting around Thailand is wonderfully easy.

Tourism Authority of Thailand Offices

HEAD OFFICE

Tourism Authority of Thailand
1600 New Phetchaburi Road,
Makkasan, Ratchathewi ,
Bangkok 10400, Thailand
telephone: +66.2.250 5500
facsimile: +66.2.250 5511
email: center@tat.or.th
website: www.tourismthailand.org

ASIA + PACIFIC

Kuala Lumpur

Tourism Authority of Thailand
Suite 22.01, 22nd Floor, Menara Citibank,
165 Jalan Ampang, 50450 Kuala Lumpur,
Malaysia
telephone: +60.3.2162 3480
facsimile: +60.3.2162 3486
email: sawatdi@po.jaring.my or tatkul@tat.or.th
areas of responsibility: Malaysia and
Brunei Darussalam

Singapore

Tourism Authority of Thailand
Royal Thai Embassy
370 Orchard Road,
Singapore 238870
telephone: +65.6235.7901
facsimile: +65.6733 5653
email: tatsin@singnet.com.sg or tatsin@tat.or.th
areas of responsibility: Singapore, Indonesia
and The Philippines

Hong Kong

Tourism Authority of Thailand
Room 1901 Jardine House,
1 Connaught Place,
Central, Hong Kong
telephone: +852.2868 0732/854
facsimile: +852.2868 4585
email: tathkg@pacific.net.hk or tathkg@tat.or.th
areas of responsibility: Hong Kong and Macau

Beijing

Tourism Authority of Thailand
Room 902, Office Tower E1, Oriental Plaza,
No.1 East Chang An Avenue,
Dong Cheng District,
Beijing, 100738, China
telephone: +86.10.8518 3526/7/8/9
facsimile: +86.10.8518 3530
email: tatbjs@tat.or.th or tatbjs@sohu.com
areas of responsibility: People's Republic of
China (except Hong Kong, Macao and
Taiwan) and Mongolia

Taipei

Thailand Tourism Division
13th Floor, Boss Tower, No 111 Sung Chiang
Road (Near Nanking East Road Junction)
Taipei 104, Taiwan
telephone: +886.2.2502 1600
facsimile: +886.2.2502 1603
email: tattpe@ms3.hinet.net or tattpe@tat.or.th
area of responsibility: Taiwan

Tokyo

Tourism Authority of Thailand
Yurakucho Denki Building, South Tower
2nd Floor, Room 259, 1-7-1 Yurakucho
Chiyoda-ku, Tokyo 100-0006, Japan
telephone: +81.3.3218 0337/55
facsimile: +81.3.3218 0655
email: tattky@tattky.com or tattky@tat.or.th
areas of responsibility: Northern Area
of Honshu Island: Tohoku and Kanto, and
Hokkaido Island

Osaka

Tourism Authority of Thailand
Technoble Yotsubashi Building, 3rd Floor,
1-6-8 Kitahorie, Nishi-ku
Osaka 550-0014, Japan
telephone: +81.6.6543 6654/5
facsimile: +81.6.6543 6660
email: info@tatosa.com
areas of responsibility: Southern Area
of Honshu Island: Kinki, Chugoku
and Chubu

Fukuoka

Tourism Authority of Thailand
EL Gala Building, 6th Floor,
1-4-2 Tenjin, Chuo-ku
Fukuoka 810-0001, Japan
telephone: +81.92.725 8808
facsimile: +81.92.735 4434
email: tatfuk@tatfuk.com or tatfuk@tat.or.th
areas of responsibility: Kyushu Island,
Shikoku Island and Okinawa

India

Tourism Authority of Thailand
Royal Thailand Embassy, 65-N, Nyaya Marg,
Chanakyapuri, New Delhi, India 110021
telephone: +91.11.2410 5408
facsimile: +91.11.2410 5409
email: tat@thaiemb.org.in or
pimkiarora@yahoo.com
areas of responsibility: India, Bangladesh,
Sri Lanka, Pakistan and Nepal

Seoul

Tourism Authority of Thailand
Coryo Daeyungak Center Building
RM. No.1205, 12th Floor, 25-5, 1-Ka,
Chungmu-Ro, Chung-Ku,
Seoul 100-706, Korea
telephone: +82.2.779 5417/771 9650
facsimile: +82.2.779 5419
email: tatsel@kornet21.net or tatsel@tat.or.th
area of responsibility: Republic of Korea

Sydney

Tourism Authority of Thailand
2nd Floor, 75 Pitt Street,
Sydney, NSW 2000 Australia
telephone: +61.2.9247 7549
facsimile: +61.2.9251 2465
email: info@thailand.net.au or tatsyd@tat.or.th
areas of responsibility: Australia, New Zealand
and South Pacific

EUROPE

London

Tourism Authority of Thailand
3rd Floor, Brook House,
98-99 Jermyn Street,
London SW1Y 6EE, England
telephone: +44.207.925 2511
facsimile: +44.207.925 2512
email: info@tat-uk.demon.co.uk or
tatuk@tat.or.th
areas of responsibility: United Kingdom,
Ireland, South Africa, Iran, Iraq, Jordan,
Lebanon, Syria and the Middle East: Bahrain,
Kuwait, Oman, Qatar, Saudi Arabia and
United Arab Emirates.

Frankfurt

Thailandisches Fremdenverkehrsamt
Bethmann Strasse 58,
D-60311 Frankfurt/M., Germany
telephone: +49.69.138 1390
facsimile: +49.69.138 13950
email: info@thailandtourismus.de or
tatfra@tat.or.th
areas of responsibility: Germany, Austria,
Slovenia, Croatia, Switzerland, Liechtenstein,
Romania, Yugoslavia[S2], Bulgaria,
Moldova, Macedonia, Albania, Czech
Republic, Slovakia, Poland, Hungary,
Bosnia-Herzegovina

Paris

Office National du Tourisme de Thailande
90, Avenue des Champs-Elysees,
75008 Paris, France
telephone: +33.1.5353 4700
facsimile: +33.1.4563 7888
email: tatpar@wanadoo.fr or tatpar@tat.or.th
areas of responsibility: France, Belgium,
Luxembourg and the Netherlands

Rome

Ente Nazionale per il Turismo Thailandese
Via Barberini 68, 4th Floor,
00187 Roma, Italy
telephone: +39.6.4201 4422/26
facsimile: +39.6.487 3500[S3]
email: tat.rome@iol.it or tatrome@tat.or.th
areas of responsibility: Italy, Spain, Greece,
Portugal, Israel, Egypt, Turkey and Cyprus

Stockholm

Tourism Authority of Thailand
Drottninggatan 33 GF,
111 51 Stockholm, Sweden
telephone: +46.8.700 5690
facsimile: +46.8.700 5699
email: info@tat.nu or tatsth@tat.or.th
areas of responsibility: Sweden, Norway,
Denmark, Finland, Iceland, Russia, Belarus,
Ukraine, Georgia, Armenia, Azerbaijan,
Kazakhstan, Uzbekistan, Turkmenistan,
Tajikistan, Kyrgyz Republic, Estonia, Latvia
and Lithuania

THE AMERICAS

Los Angeles

Tourism Authority of Thailand
611 North Larchmont Boulevard, 1st Floor,
Los Angeles, CA 90004,
United States of America
telephone: +1.323.461 9814
facsimile: +1.323.461 9834
email: tatla@ix.netcom.com or tatla@tat.or.th
areas of responsibility: Alaska, Arizona,
California, Colorado, Hawaii, Idaho,
Kansas, Montana, Nebraska, Nevada,
New Mexico, North Dakota, Oklahoma,
Oregon, South Dakota, Texas, Utah,
Washington, Wyoming, Guam Island and
all Central and South American Countries

New York

Tourism Authority of Thailand
61 Broadway, Suite 2810
New York, N.Y. 10006,
United States of America
telephone: +1.212.432 0433
facsimile: +1.212.269 2588
email: info@tatny.com or tatny@tat.or.th
areas of responsibility: Alabama, Arkansas,
Connecticut, Delaware, Florida, Georgia,
Illinois, Indiana, Iowa, Kentucky, Louisiana,
Maine, Maryland, Massachusetts, Michigan,
Minnesota, Mississippi, Missouri, New York,
New Hampshire, New Jersey, North Carolina,
Ohio, Pennsylvania, Rhode Island,
South Carolina, Tennessee, Vermont, Virginia,
Washington D.C., West Virginia,
Wisconsin, Puerto Rico, the Bahamas and
Canada Countries (West Canada: Alberta,
British Columbia, Manitoba, Northwest
Territories, Saskatchewan and Yukon;
East Canada: Ontario, Quebec, New
Brunswick, Nova Scotia and Newfoundland)

Thailand

HAPPINESS ON EARTH

hotels • restaurants • shops • spas

thailandchic

hotels • restaurants • shops • spas

thailandchic

text chami jotisalikorn • annette tan

ARCHIPELAGO PRESS

managing editor
melisa teo

consultant editor
yvan van outrive

editor
michelle ooi

designers
lisa damayanti • nelani jinadasa

production manager
sin kam cheong

first published in 2006 by
editions didier millet pte ltd
121 telok ayer street, #03-01
singapore 068590
edm@edmbooks.com.sg
www.edmbooks.com

©2006 editions didier millet pte ltd

Printed in Singapore

All rights reserved. No part of this publication may be
reproduced, stored in a retrieval system, or transmitted in
any form or by any means, electronic, electrostatic, magnetic
tape, mechanical, photocopying, recording or otherwise,
without prior written permission from the publisher.

isbn: 981-4155-03-9

COVER CAPTIONS:

1–3: *Costa Lanta, Krabi.*
4: *One of Ayutthaya's many temples.*
5: *Contemporary Thai design showcased at the catwalks of Bangkok's fashion shows.*
6: *Elephant polo.*
7: *Vertigo Grill and Moon Bar.*
8: *Snorkelling in southern Thailand.*
9: *Phuket.*
10: *Lotus flowers.*
11, 13, THIS PAGE AND OPPOSITE: *Stylish details and floral bath at Anantara Resort and Spa.*
12: *Pool at Srilanta.*
14 AND 18: *Flora at i.sawan Residential Spa and Club.*
15–16: *Kirimaya Golf Resort and Spa.*
17: *Jim Thompson Thai silk.*
19: *The Chedi Chiang Mai.*
20–22: *Mandarin Oriental Dhara Dhevi.*
PAGE 2: *Sunset at Sukhothai.*
PAGE 6: *View of pool at Evason Phuket Resort and Six Senses Spa.*
PAGE 8 AND 9: *Bangkok at night.*

contents

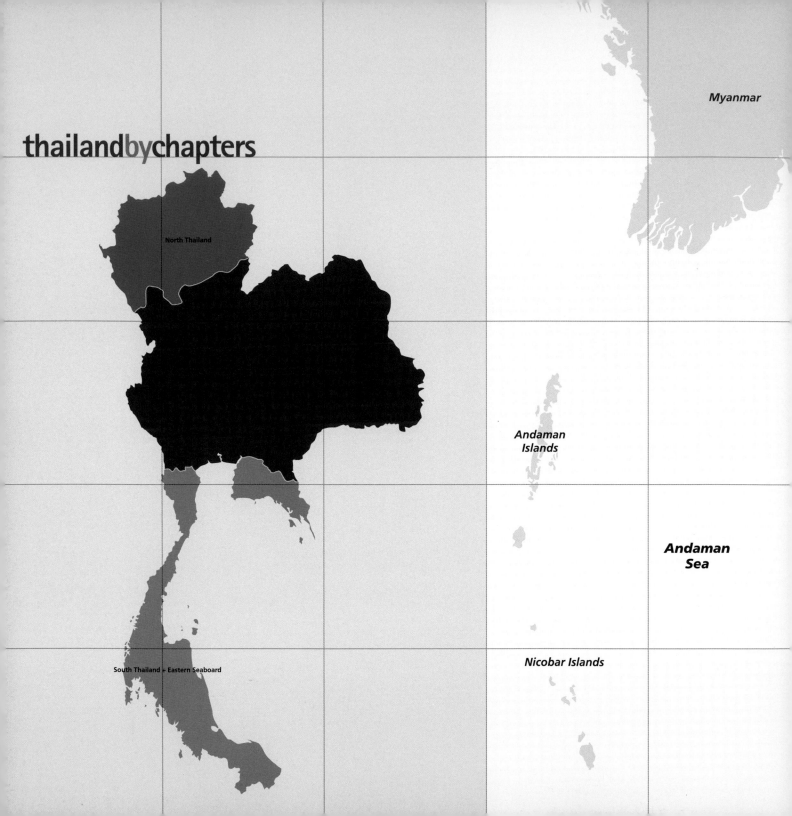

thailandbychapters

North Thailand

South Thailand + Eastern Seaboard

Myanmar

Andaman
Islands

Andaman
Sea

Nicobar Islands

thailandbyprovinces

China

Laos

...onphanom

...roen

...ul

Vietnam

Kanchanaburi

...Nburi

Ratburi

...ongkhram

Phetchaburi

...burng ...Chanthaburi

Cambodia

Prachuap Khiri Khan

Gulf of Thailand

Chumphon

Ran...

Suratthani

Phang Nga

...Nakhonsithammarat

Krabi

Phuket

Phatthalung

Trang

Satun Songkhla

Pattani

Malaysia ...arathiwat

introduction

thailand: the land of the free

What is it that makes Thailand one of the most vibrant, energetic, and creative nations in Asia today? Aside from its magnificent landscapes and lush fertility, Thailand's history and culture reflect the rich artistic heritage of a magnificent kingdom. The kingdom's identity continues to thrive and evolve, not just by adapting to contemporary trends but also making its own imprint on the world today.

What gives Thailand such a strong presence in the region? For one thing, Thailand has the distinction of being the only country in Southeast Asia that was never colonised by a foreign power. There were repeated invasion attempts by the Burmese in ancient times, and a brief Japanese occupation in WWII, but for the most part, Thailand has always been, like its name, the Land of the Free.

Thailand evaded European colonisation thanks to the intelligence of her rulers, who tolerated foreigners, played them off against one another, and traded outlying lands in Laos and Cambodia to safeguard Thai independence. While maintaining an attitude of openness to foreign cultures, the Thai nation has always retained its own strong sense of identity and cultural pride.

Thai people possess a spirit of patriotism and independence, as well as great zest for life. Their reverence for all its forms is manifest in the gentle compassion given to animals and other human beings, and to the passion exhibited in food, arts, faith and work.

the thai smile

The famous Thai smile that gave the country its name, the Land of Smiles, characterises its friendly, good-natured people. One of their most distinctive traits is their sense of fun—a characteristic which they call sanuk and the French refer to as joie de vivre. Thai people have a natural cheerfulness and light-hearted spirit that imbues everything they do. Even at work, there is a sense of fun, plenty of teasing and genuine feelings of warmth among colleagues that make life perpetually enjoyable. And why not smile all day? In Thailand, life really is good and enjoyable. The culture is a social one, with

THIS PAGE (FROM TOP): Bangkok is a mix of modern metropolis and old-world splendour; a relentless sense of fun typifies the famous Thai charm.

OPPOSITE: Lotus ponds greet the eye all across the country.

a tradition of extended family and community, and a society where extreme importance is placed on one's manners and speech towards others. Because of their great love of community, Thai people revel in social interaction, loud noise and hustle and bustle. In contrast to the European outlook, the thought of being alone, or travelling and dining solo in a foreign land, is deemed a sad affair for the kindred-loving Thai.

Thai people are renowned for their gentleness and politeness in any situation. The deeper implication, and more socially significant side of the Thai smile, is that it is a gracious way of 'saving face', or avoiding embarrassment and loss of dignity. Smiling covers up any potentially negative or distressing situation. Thai people shun any sort of confrontation, argument or conflict, and will go to great lengths to avoid it, to the point that they hardly ever say no, even when they mean it. They simply answer affirmatively and carry on as before. Any question is always answered with a yes, even if the answer is otherwise. "Do you have some bananas?" "Yes. We have no bananas."

A key element of Thai culture is great respect for religion, the monarchy, elders, and family. At each social stratum, from the humblest servant to the loftiest aristocrat, Thai people practise a natural politeness and grace that is unfailingly appealing and always pleasant. Thai culture reveres the head as the highest and most sacred part of the body. So in Thailand, one never touches another person's head—this is considered shockingly rude. It is also disrespectful to have your head higher than the head of an elder or your boss, or someone of a higher social class, which is why Thai manners are so deferential, with lots of bowing and nodding in social interactions. Correspondingly, the foot is considered the lowliest part of the body; it is the height of rudeness to point your foot at someone, or touch another person with your feet.

Another way of showing respect in Thai culture is by keeping good personal hygiene and being properly dressed. Thai people shudder at the thought of venturing out in public shoddily groomed or shabbily attired, as it results in loss of face and is disrespectful to other people. Due to the tropical heat, Thai people usually shower and powder themselves two or three times a day. When meeting elders or officials, they always dress modestly as a sign of respect. Thai people enjoy dressing up and going out because it adds sanuk to the custom of being well groomed; this also appeals to their love of visual arts, creative flair and social interaction. It's no wonder there is a such passion for following fashion trends in Thailand.

With all of these social customs stemming from a reverence for fun, behaviour and respect, the service industry is exceptionally brilliant in Thailand, with its signature warmth unrivalled by any other country. Visitors become addicted to Thailand and her people.

festivals + fun

Sanuk is apparent in the numerous festivals and pageants all year long throughout the country. In fact, there's at least one, and sometimes two, public holidays every month. The only months without public holidays in Thailand are June and September.

The favourite and biggest festival is Songkran, the water-throwing event celebrating

the Thai New Year in mid-April, during the most scorching week of the year. There is no religious significance to this festival — it's just a fun, cooling way to usher in the New Year. The whole country can join in. In Bangkok and Chiang Mai, revellers ride around in pick-up trucks with buckets of water and giant water guns to douse all passers-by amidst shrieks of delight.

One of the most beautiful festivals is Loy Krathong. Celebrated during November's full moon season, small floral floats made of banana leaves and flowers, decorated with incense and candles, are sent with wishes down rivers and streams. It is a lovely sight to behold and strikes a romantic, magical note when celebrated among the moonlit ruins of Ayutthaya and Sukhothai.

Some of the most colourful festivals are held in the rural northeast. At the Yasothon Rocket Festival, rockets are launched in wild abandon, accompanied by a raucous parade abounding in giant fertility symbols to bring rain to the crops. Another unique event is the Phii Takon Festival, one of the wildest festivals held in the northeastern Loei

province. Participants don exquisitely painted 'spirit' masks and carry fertility symbols in a parade. This festival commemorates a Buddhist legend where Buddha is greeted by a gang of spirits upon returning to his hometown, before reaching enlightenment.

spirituality: the centre of life

The Thai calendar is peppered with religious holidays honouring all the major events in the life of Buddha. Reverence for the Buddhist faith is one of the strongest tenets of Thai culture, and pervades all aspects of behaviour and thought. This is evident in the sheer number of temples in every city or village. No Thai community, be it a metropolitan

THIS PAGE: *Wat Phra Si Sanphet's three imposing stupas have become the symbol of the ancient capital of Ayutthaya.*

OPPOSITE (FROM TOP): *Ordination into the monkhood is a rite of passage for every Thai male; well-kept spirit houses on the premises of homes and offices provide mini-dwellings for the spirits of the land.*

hub or a rural village, is complete without the presence of a temple to serve society. In traditional societies, the temple is at the heart of life, playing many roles as religious centre, healing centre, school, orphanage, meeting ground, playground, the venue of village fairs, festivals—and even a place to take homeless animals.

The Thai people's peacefulness and calm disposition is thought to stem from their strong ties to the Buddhist faith, which places emphasis on mindfulness, non-violence and compassion. Thai people believe in acquiring merit in this life to ensure that during their next rebirth, they are reincarnated in a better life. Hope for a good reincarnation is obtained by making offerings at the temple, giving alms to monks, or, in the case of males, becoming a monk for a short period. In Thai culture, every male is expected to assume monkhood at some point in his life. Monkhood is not a fixed state, and can last from one week to as long as one chooses. It used to be a rite of passage between the time a man finished school and started a career, or got married. These days, a period of monkhood is often undertaken when a parent has passed away, to make merit for the deceased as well as the rest of one's family.

spirit houses

A feature unique to Thai culture is the 'spirit house', surrounded by offerings of flowers, incense and food, and visible in many homes and office buildings. Spirit houses are usually elaborate little structures resembling miniature wooden houses or, in the case of office buildings, cement constructions imitating Khmer temples.

Thai people believe that the land is protected by guardian spirits, so when a new house or building is erected, the human occupants must provide a spirit house for the spirits to live in. Daily offerings must be made to keep them happy. In return, the spirits will protect the occupants and bring them peace and security. In the case of office buildings, it is hoped that the spirits will bring financial success.

Spirit houses should not be neglected, otherwise the disgruntled and hungry spirits may decide to stir up mischief or bring bad luck to the premises!

native healing traditions and wellness

The spiritual traditions of Thailand have helped set off the Asian spa quake, with Thai spas at the epicentre. Their incredible appeal is linked to the country's unique healing traditions, in which mental and spiritual well-being is derived from Buddhist practices that have been part of Thai life for centuries.

In Thailand, the unique treatments offered in spas today are derived from ancient Thai rituals of natural healing, such as the traditional healing massage, herbal baths and compresses. These soothing methods were developed from ancient Indian Ayurvedic medicine that migrated from India with Buddhist missionary monks in the 2nd and 3rd centuries. Monks were the healers during those times. And even now, modern herbal body treatments are formulated from centuries-old native health and beauty customs.

Thai spa treatments are performed with the innate gentleness and warmth that the Thai people are so renowned for. It is the extra dimension of caring in the Thai spa experience which makes you feel so delightfully pampered.

Thai spa locations have an enormous impact on visitors. Many Thai spas are set in exotic beach and mountain environments with gorgeous natural surroundings, making the whole spa experience so special. They are increasingly creative and sophisticated in their interior design too. Some spas feature impressive design concepts that you won't find in other countries. Thailand is indeed home to a wide range of spa styles and services, ranging from the ultra-luxurious to the rustic basic.

food fusion in true thai style

At the heart of Thai culture is food, glorious food. It is no mystery why the Thai nation is so obsessed with good eating when the cuisine is simply brimming with variety and flavour.

Eating is not confined to three meals a day in Thailand. Instead, the joyful act is meant to encompass snacking in-between, and indeed at all times! Why not, when the country boasts an incredible range of appetisers and food items to be enjoyed all day long?

Visitors to Thailand marvel at the abundance, diversity and incredible flavours of Thai cooking, which runs from humble country fare to unique royal gastronomy. Many people visit Thailand just for its remarkable food.

Thai dishes have absorbed influences from India and China, yet the food of Thailand has preserved the distinctive cuisines of its own regions. Aside from its famous fragrant curries, one of the distinguishing aspects of Thai cuisine is its use of fresh herbal ingredients that have become globally famous. Lemongrass, lime, coriander, fish sauce and chillies have established themselves as the icons of Thai cooking, imparting their blend of distinctive flavours. Thai cuisine is, without a doubt, the trend in hip restaurants and cookbooks around the world today.

THIS PAGE (FROM TOP): Food-stall dining is a delicious way to experience Thai cooking; fruit carving is a traditional and intriguing Thai art; many popular Thai dishes are influenced by Chinese cuisine.

OPPOSITE (FROM TOP): Enjoy some body pampering in elegant Thai-style salas; prakop is a traditional Thai herbal poultice used to soothe muscle aches and pains.

a lasting design tradition

Thailand's arts and architectural heritage reached dazzling heights of splendour through royal patronage over the centuries. The gilded opulence and glittering spires of classic temple architecture were developed during the Ayutthaya and Rattanakosin eras, so these structures were true reflections of the country's prosperous kingdoms.

Thai Buddha images can be identified by their stylised forms and serenity of expression. The earlier statues were influenced by two sources—the voluptuous curves of the Greco-style Gandhara images from India, and the heavy-set ones with blocky heads and heavy lips from Khmer art. But over the centuries, Thai Buddha images forged their own stylistic identity. The epitome of pure Thai sculptural-style is the Sukhothai Buddha, with its distinct elongated, curved face and figure, arched eyebrows and long, pointed nose. The overall display evokes a sinuous androgyny that seems more abstract than corporeal. The Sukhothai style is also known for initiating the walking Buddha figure, a departure from the traditional seated and standing forms that preceded it.

The customary Thai motifs are unique. The triangle is a favourite, often integrated into all aspects of design, as shown by the steeply gabled roofs of traditional wooden houses, the inward slopes of cabinets, and classic triangular pillows. Variations of the triangle and diamond are also played out in ceramics, woodcarving, mother-of-pearl inlay and textiles. The lai krajang is a motif of pointed leaves made from geometric shapes like interlocking diamonds, hexagons and octagons. Flames and the holy lotus flower are also dominant in Thai décor. The kinetic flame pattern known as lai kranok is often seen on temples, ceramics and textiles.

With its profusion of exotic blooms, it is only natural that floral décor, another of Thailand's outstanding art forms, features prominently in the country's design tradition. Flower arrangement is an intrinsic part of the decorative arts, evident in the jasmine garlands or puangmalai sold on the streets and in temples as religious offerings, and

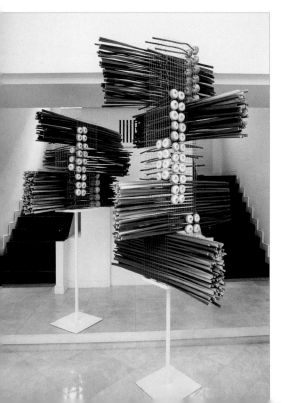

welcome garlands. In the old days, the art of threading flower garlands was passed down through generations of Thai women, along with fruit carving and cooking. The pretty garlands can be simple or elaborate—the latter involving creations woven in kranok and krajang motifs to celebrate royal ceremonies and rituals.

contemporary thai chic

In food, fashion, art and décor, Thailand is leading the wave of contemporary Asian style. If you want a barometer of the importance of style in Thailand today, you have only to look at any newsstand. There are scores of magazines devoted to many lifestyle issues, and they're not just in Thai; other international titles jostle for space with local publications. The Thai-language editions of *Elle* and *Elle Décor* are two of the most popular magazines in Bangkok. In recent years, titles such as *Cosmopolitan*, *Esquire*, *Cleo*, *Marie Claire*, *Madame Figaro* and *Harper's Bazaar* have launched hugely popular Thai-language editions, too, with a mixture of Thai and international feature stories on trends, cuisine and décor.

The Thai nation has always been able to assimilate external influences whilst still protecting its unique cultural identity. Masters of mimicry, Thai artisans experiment with foreign inspirations and can produce something singularly Thai with a twist, or—on the flip side—something blatantly foreign with a dash of Thai. A good example is Thai-Western fusion food like Spaghetti Pla Khem or spaghetti served with traditional Thai salted fish and chilli instead of Italian tomato sauce. Or green bread flavoured with fragrant pandanus leaf—a favourite Thai herbal flavouring.

The visitors who flock to Thailand and fall in love with its landscape, culture, arts and cuisine have helped bring many things Thai into global consciousness. Thai style is

THIS PAGE: Thai designers keep setting the bar even higher with innovative décor features. This unusual vertical garden grows above the bar of a chic Bangkok restaurant.

OPPOSITE (FROM TOP): Puangmalai is the traditional pretty floral garland used for religious offerings and greetings; a sinuous walking Buddha from the Sukhothai period; contemporary floral design is breaking new ground in the Thai arts scene.

making its mark across the world. What began as the spread of Thai influences in hip cuisine has expanded to include contemporary décor and fashion, thanks to a talented crop of Thai designers carving their niche on the international scene. Jim Thompson Thai silk is known the world over for its luxurious, shimmering qualities, while furniture designer Ou Bhaholyodhin and fashion designer Nagara are crafting of-the-moment looks inspired by classic Thai forms and garments. Their collections are being snapped up by locals and foreigners in hot pursuit of modern Asian chic.

Thailand's bounty of skilled craftsmanship and yen for fashion are taking wing in the government's Bangkok Fashion City campaign. Promoting Thai fashion in the world market, the campaign sponsors international fashion shows and spotlights the creations of top Thai labels like Nagara, Metta, Greyhound, Senada, Kloset, Anurak, Zenith, Tube Gallery, Fly Now, Mae Fah Luang, Abnormal and Tango.

THIS PAGE (CLOCKWISE FROM TOP):
Bangkok Fashion Week 2005;
contemporary northern art by
Angkarn Kalyanapong;
the city's boutique interiors are
as varied as the merchandise;
OPPOSITE: Princess Siriwanwaree
Nareeratana (in black gown)
acknowledges the applause
for her debut collection.

a blossoming arts scene

The Thailand arts focus is shifting from traditional to contemporary. Thai artists have only recently gained international visibility. Two of the country's most celebrated modern artists, Araya Rasdjarmrernsook and the late Montien Boonma, were represented in the 2005 Venice Biennale, the world's most prestigious international art show.

The 1990s financial boom led to a real-estate boom, with the newly moneyed becoming interested in contemporary Thai art as a means of enlivening their walls and making good investments. This fed the thriving art scene in Bangkok, with art parties and media attention turning emerging artists into local celebrities.

In Bangkok, aside from the many galleries specialising in the works of modern Thai and Asian artists, such as Carpe Diem Galleries, Gallery 55, Surapon Gallery, and Akko Collection House, there is now a trend in art restaurants and pubs. These outlets showcase the productions of local painters both for décor and for sale. Collectors from Singapore and Hong Kong have started buying contemporary Southeast Asian works in Bangkok, and will often look to make investments in Thai artists.

Thai style is making its mark across the world.

bangkok+centralplains +northeastthailand

Myanmar

Laos

Udon Thani

Sakonnakhon

Phetchabun

Nakhon Ratchasima

Phanom Rung Historical Park (Buriram)

Surin

Srisaket

Khao Phra Viharn

Ayuthaya

Cambodia

Gulf of Thailand

southeast asia's capital of chic

Just how did Bangkok get to be Southeast Asia's capital of chic? The bustling, dusty metropolis will never win prizes for Most Beautiful City, compared to its more orderly neighbours like Singapore or Kuala Lumpur. But the City of Angels has no rivals when it comes to charisma, energy, history, food, fashion, funk, quirk and adventure. In Bangkok, all these elements are meshed together in a dizzying mêlée, so that ancient traditions merge with cutting-edge attitudes, and old-world charm is alive and dressed in the latest international fashions.

Transcending the chaos is the famous Thai joy of life. The locals' sense of fun and joie de vivre celebrate all things that make life enjoyable. Heavenly food, classy design, fun fashion and beauty are all embraced wholeheartedly. The result is an appreciation for all things bright and beautiful—welcome to the world of Bangkok chic.

the chakri dynasty

The story of Bangkok is inextricably linked to the Chakri dynasty, the Thai kingdom's current ruling family. As their royal patrons of art and culture, Thai people today have the early Chakri monarchs to thank for envisioning and bringing to life the dazzling grandeur of the city's historic palaces and temples.

Bangkok was founded in 1782 at the inception of the Chakri dynasty. After the destruction of Ayutthaya by the Burmese, General Taksin made himself the king and established a new capital down-river in Thonburi. But Taksin eventually showed signs of madness and was executed by one of his generals.

This general, Chao Phraya Chakri, in turn put himself on the throne. During his reign, he moved the capital across the river to where present-day Bangkok stands. Chao Phraya Chakri and his successor took it upon themselves to restore the glorious culture that was wiped away with Ayutthaya's destruction. The third Chakri king, Phra Nang Klao, initiated trade with the Chinese and invented a new royal title system, which bestowed the title 'Rama' upon the kings of the dynasty. He became Rama III.

THIS PAGE (FROM TOP): *Modern office buildings tower above the Chong Non Si intersection on Sathorn Road; 'fashion forward' is the code of living for Bangkok trendsetters.*
OPPOSITE: *Bangkok's Grand Palace embodies all the glamour and mystique of the exotic orient.*

His successor, Rama IV—better known as King Mongkut—had been a monk for 27 years, ascending the throne in 1851. One of the most enlightened of the Chakri kings, he opened diplomatic and trade relations with Western nations. Adept in Pali, Sanskrit, Latin and English, he hired an English teacher for his children, the legendary Anna Leonowens. She wrote the book *An English Governess in the Court of Siam*, now the basis of a Broadway musical and two Hollywood movies. The first movie catapulted Mongolian actor Yul Brynner to international stardom as the bald-headed King of Siam. A recent remake cast Chinese superstar Chao Yun Fat as the king and American actress Jodie Foster as Anna. The costumes were gorgeous in both movies.

King Mongkut had numerous wives and 77 children. One of his sons, Chulalongkorn, became Rama V, and reigned from 1868 to 1910. Considered to be one of the greatest Chakri kings, he followed in his father's footsteps and implemented many legal and administrative reforms. He abolished slavery, constructed railways, established a civil service and restructured the legal code. He maintained diplomatic relations with European powers. And by successfully trading what once were the Thai territories of Laos and Cambodia to the French, and Burma (now Myanmar) to the British, he evaded the colonisation that befell the rest of Southeast Asia.

His British-educated son, King Vajiravudh, made educational reforms during his reign from 1910 to 1925, and brought about compulsory education. He adopted European practices for the country, changing the Thai Buddhist calendar to the Western calendar, and instituting the use of surnames for all Thai citizens. Thailand's long history of military coups began during King Vajiravudh's reign in 1912, a political pattern that still dogs the country even to this day.

In 1932, when his brother King Prajadhipok was on the throne, a major coup was carried out by a group of Thai students who had studied in Paris. This coup successfully abolished absolute monarchy and led to the development of a constitutional monarchy, similar to that of Britain. The king abdicated in 1935 and lived in exile in England. Childless, he named his nephew as his successor. This new king was 10-year-old Ananda Mahidol, then living and studying in Switzerland.

In the meantime, political power was in the firm hands of a military leader named Phibul Songkhram, who had been involved in the 1932 coup. During this time, the country's name was changed from Siam to Thailand, meaning Land of the Free. However, the 20-year-old King Mahidol, who had returned to Thailand in 1945 to ascend the throne after completing his studies, was tragically shot dead in his bedroom a year later. To this very day, the circumstances of the young king's untimely death remain shrouded in mystery and though conspiracy theories abound, the matter is never spoken of in public and no public explanation was ever given.

THIS PAGE: *Monarchs of the currently reigning Chakri Dynasty are commemorated in these statues at the Grand Palace in Bangkok.*
OPPOSITE: *Hundreds of devoted subjects flocked to pay their last respects at the royal funeral of Thailand's Princess Mother.*

His 19-year-old brother, Bhumibhol Adulyadej, became King Rama IX and is the country's most beloved king, revered by Thai citizens for his kindness and devotion to public good works. Portraits of the king and queen grace every household and office in Thailand, and his birthday on December 5 is celebrated as the country's national day, as well as Father's Day. The queen's birthday, on August 12, is Mother's Day in Thailand. Bhumibhol Adulyadej is the world's longest reigning monarch.

ratanakosin style: architecture and the arts

When Rama I moved his new capital to Bangkok in 1782, he called it Ratanakosin Inayothaya, meaning 'place for precious gems', because it was the new home for the beautiful Emerald Buddha. Since then, the name Ratanakosin has come to refer to the present period, or Bangkok period, in Thai history. Part of the Grand Palace complex by the river, the Temple of the Emerald Buddha is the most sacred temple in Thailand.

The temples of this period were built on a grand scale to showcase the dawn of a new era. The variety of stylistic influences was mostly due to the personal preferences of the different rulers. Early Ratanakosin temples reflected the Ayutthaya style. But by the early 19th century, under Rama III's reign, Thailand had stabilised, waging fewer wars and gaining more trading contacts with China. This increased interaction brought Chinese style to Thailand, evident in temple architecture like the prang at Wat Arun, the famous Temple of Dawn. Chinese dragons and griffins replaced traditional Thai gable decorations, and temples were adorned with bright Chinese ceramic fragments.

The Ratanakosin era is also known for its murals—perhaps because these are the best surviving examples of Thai painting from that time. The basic themes in temple murals incorporate religious scenes from Buddha's life, although depictions of the *Ramayana* epic can be seen in the Grand Palace, and paintings of local life are also common for the period. Chinese art motifs were adopted and the images of foreigners who came to Thailand were depicted in murals too. Great strides in the art of Thai painting were made during Rama II's reign, and many works are evident at Wat Po.

THIS PAGE (FROM TOP): Naga heads are a key design motif on the spectacular temples of Bangkok's Grand Palace; Buddha images viewed through the stained-glass window of a Bangkok shop.

OPPOSITE (FROM LEFT): Stone Garuda-head details on Wat Arun; Wat Arun's imposing spires cast a mystical skyscape on the Bangkok riverside.

King Mongkut brought about a return to traditional Thai forms. During his rule, the Western style of depicting three-dimensional perspectives was added to the traditional Thai way of painting two-dimensional perspectives, creating new complexities in the murals of his era. The finest examples were produced by a monk named Khrua in Kong, the first Thai to adopt Western-style painting. His work can be seen at Wat Rajapradit and Wat Bowarniwet in the Ratanakosin Island area of Bangkok.

Ayutthaya-style sculptures continued into the Ratanakosin era. It was also during King Mongkut's reign that the Buddha sculptures began to shed their glamorous jewels and become more natural-looking, sans royal regalia. His son Chulalongkorn, who was influenced by the West, erected monasteries incorporating the Western style—including stained-glass windows and the Gothic style in some Bangkok temples. Aside from the collection at Bangkok's National Museum, exquisite Thai artwork can be appreciated in the private Prasart Museum, located in the suburbs of Bangkok. The museum is comprised of a replica of a royal residence and examples of various classic Thai buildings, boasting a collection of royal furniture and jewellery of exquisite quality.

THIS PAGE (FROM TOP): Inside Wat Mahathat, one of the country's most revered temples; this royal top-knot crown is a stunning example of Thailand's exquisite decorative traditions.

OPPOSITE: Bangkok's beautiful Grand Palace is the esteemed site of the sacred Temple of the Emerald Buddha.

temple traditions

The fabulous temples and buildings of the early Ratanakosin era are grouped together in an area known as Ratanakosin Island, so called because the area lies between two large canals running parallel to the river, making it resemble an island.

Many regard the Grand Palace and Temple of the Emerald Buddha as the apogee of Thai architecture. Construction first began in 1787, but new buildings have been gradually added over the past 200 years. The end result is an eclectic collection of various architectural styles from past centuries.

The early buildings followed the Ayutthaya style, but the taste for Western culture became evident in the mid-19th century with the Phra Thinang Chakri Mahaprasat. The royal residence combines a Western neoclassic body with a classic Thai roof and royal spire. Construction began in 1875, supervised by two English architects.

Many regard the Grand Palace...as the apogee of Thai architecture.

The most stunning of the royal buildings is the romantic and elegant Phra Thinang Dusit Mahaprasat, erected during Rama I's reign. A stately white building topped with a four-tier saddle roof and seven-tier royal spire, it is considered the finest illustration of traditional symbolic architecture in Thailand. The royal family lived in the Grand Palace until the early 20th century, when King Chulalongkorn built a new royal abode called Chitrlada Palace in the European style. Chitrlada Palace was built at a new site in Bangkok called Dusit, and remains the official residence of the royal family to this day. The Grand Palace still functions as a living palace, though, and provides the venue for royal ceremonies, coronations, funerals, as well as state receptions and banquets. It stands as an epitome of Thai cultural traditions.

Every palace had to have a temple in its compound, and so Rama I instructed the construction of Wat Phra Kaew to shelter the Emerald Buddha. The temple buildings are covered with coloured glass and gleaming gold, remaining to this day as elaborate examples of Ratanakosin style at its most outstanding. The patterns on the walls make use of classic Thai motifs, while the temple's exquisite and completely restored murals depict the *Ramakien*, the Thai version of the Indian epic, the *Ramayana*. These murals were painted during Rama I's reign.

Although there are thousands of temples to be found around Bangkok, especially in the Ratanakosin Island area, two temples stand out in terms of their Thai architecture and design.

Wat Po is not only one of the most picturesque temples in Thailand, it is also the oldest and biggest in Bangkok, possessing the largest reclining Buddha and the most extensive collection of Buddhas in the whole of Thailand. The beauty of the mother-of-pearl inlay adorning the reclining Buddha figure is breathtaking. Dating back from the 16th century, the style of Wat Po has the classic signs of Chinese influence, with tell-tale glazed ceramic décor evident on the stupas and temple buildings, as well as many Chinese-accented stone figures of people and animals dotted around the temple compound.

Wat Arun, or the Temple of Dawn, is one of the most popular postcard images of Thailand, with its silhouette dominating the riverside. The temple was constructed in the 19th century during the reigns of Rama II and Rama III. It has a style all its own, with a Khmer-influenced prang elongated into a typically Thai curving shape, instead of the traditional Khmer rounded tower shape. Covered with broken and glazed Chinese porcelain, the prang further embodies Chinese architectural influences of the time. When illuminated at night or for festivals, the temple's splendour reaches new heights.

classic houses: thai design for living

Aside from temples, the most distinctive form of Thai architecture is the elegantly gabled Thai house. While variations exist in the North and South, Central Plains houses are the quintessence of the style, developed from the needs of an agrarian society.

Since Thai communities traditionally revolved around waterways, people lived in houses built on stilts, or in houseboats. And because river plains flooded during the monsoon, even inland houses were built on stilts. Their inward sloping walls helped brace the wooden building against the floods, and the stilts created a sheltered space below for housing animals, farming implements and carts.

All houses had large outdoor verandas, where eating and social activities took place under shady trees. Built without nails, the lattice wood panelling of the houses was fitted together like a jigsaw puzzle, so homes could be taken apart and then reassembled when necessary. Since Thai houses are built according to strict rules of dimension, they are perfectly proportioned, from humble farmers' homes to grand royal residences. The adorning flame-like curl—the chor fa—is the most classic of Thai décor motifs. Seen on both houses and temples, it adds great beauty to functional designs.

The Thai house theme is a popular décor concept in hotels, restaurants, spas and boutiques around the country, and a lasting symbol of cultural identity. Alas, classic houses have almost vanished from the scene in Bangkok, and are now simply kept as garden novelties in private homes or museums.

THIS PAGE: The elegantly pointed roofs of classic Thai houses.

OPPOSITE (FROM TOP): Built by King Chulalongkorn, the royal throne hall is still used for audiences with the reigning monarch; the detail of an ogre on the murals depicts the Ramakien legend in the Grand Palace; the powerful grace and size of the giant Reclining Buddha at Bangkok's Wat Po is nothing short of awe-inspiring.

THIS PAGE (FROM LEFT): *The legendary Jim Thompson House Museum in Bangkok displays the late owner's extensive Asian antiques and art collection; the museum is a tribute to classic Thai architecture.*

OPPOSITE (FROM TOP): *Balls of silk yarn framed by shimmering Thai silk curtains at the Jim Thompson House; a vestibule leading to the master bedroom at the Kukrit Pramoj House Museum in Bangkok.*

'the house on the klong'

The most famous Thai house museum in Bangkok is Jim Thompson's house. It nestles in a tiny lane opposite the National Stadium and the bustling MBK shopping mall. Locals call it "the house on the klong". This was the home of the legendary American textiles businessman Jim Thompson, who lived in Thailand during the 1950s. He is credited with single-handedly reviving the Thai silk industry, which was then in serious decline. Jim Thompson brought Thai silk to the attention of the international fashion world and founded the company bearing his name.

The museum showcases his collection of Thai and Southeast Asian arts and antiques, including extensive examples of Thai ceramics and paintings. A later addition is the textile museum, exhibiting Thai national and regional textiles and costumes. There is a sizeable exhibition hall and a contemporary Thai-style restaurant, serving food reminiscent of the dinner parties that Jim Thompson was so famous for hosting. Set in a lush tropical garden, Jim Thompson's House is a glamorous high-society venue for many of Bangkok's most elegant private parties, dinners, launch events and weddings.

m. l. kukrit pramoj's house

This was the private home of M. L. Kukrit Pramoj, one of Thailand's most prominent statesmen. A former Prime Minister, author and patron of the arts, he lived in this house until his death in 1995. It stands as a large residential compound in what is now the central business district of the modern metropolis. The sight of its classic Thai gabled roof juxtaposed against a Sathorn Road skyscraper is a typical image of old-meets-new in contemporary Bangkok.

The residence is actually a collection of many different Thai buildings, including a huge open-air reception hall pavilion in the garden area with a pretty lotus pond and expansive lawn. Now a museum, the location is a popular venue for chic social events and private functions—especially when party organisers are looking for a classic Thai setting in a convenient location.

suan pakkad palace

Once the home of a royal prince and now a museum, the name of Suan Pakkad means 'cabbage garden' in Thai, and the palace is located on the grounds of what used to be a commercial vegetable garden. This was the residence of Prince Chumbhot of Nagara Svarga, a grandson of King Chulalongkorn, or Rama V. The property is a complex of six large Thai houses from different parts of Central Thailand, and home to a lovely collection of Buddha sculptures and royal furniture. The highlight of them all is the Lacquer Pavilion, a Thai-style house made from awesome black and gold lacquer. The pavilion is believed to date from the Ayutthaya period and remains an impressive example of exquisite lacquer artistry, depicting scenes from the life of Buddha, and the lives of people from that era.

thai cuisine and eating out in bangkok

Bangkok food is the food of the Central Plains, and its most unique aspect is the royal cuisine. Royal cuisine, with dishes made from rare or complex ingredients, was the speciality of the women of the palace and aristocratic households. Great skill was required in blending and preparing these recipes, meaning hours or even days of chopping, grinding and carving. Royal cuisine had subtler and more delicate flavours than normal food. Some dishes have made it into everyday cooking, such as mee grob, a crispy, sweet-and-sour rice noodle dish; and look choop, a dessert made of bean paste and coconut milk and shaped into exquisite miniature fruits, similar to European marzipan confectionery.

Beautiful presentation was a feature of royal cooking. The art of fruit and vegetable carving was a skill taught to aristocratic ladies, who carved elaborate filigree patterns from cucumbers, melons, pumpkins and other fruits. Royal cuisine is now served in top restaurants and hotels in Bangkok—excellent venues for formal and business dining.

Chinese food has become a part of Bangkok's cuisine as much as ethnic Chinese people have become part of the Thai nation. When Chinese immigrants first settled as merchants and farmers in this part of Asia, their food also made its way over. Many of the noodle dishes found in Thai cooking are Chinese in origin, as well as stir-fried recipes with duck, pork and beancurd, and some types of dim sum.

Bangkok is known for all the best that Thai food has to offer—and has a fantastic range of international cuisine as well. Thailand's capital city is a food lover's paradise. With the Thai love of eating and an openness to international trends, Bangkok lends itself perfectly to many fusion food menus and trendy eateries with a spectrum of style concepts, ambience and décor. You can find beloved Thai food classics presented in chic contemporary settings like Galapapruek at Emporium; Face; Curries and More in Soi Ruam Rudee; and Tea for Two at the bustling and trendy Siam Centre .

Sometimes Thai food takes on nouvelle elements. Old favourites blend with new ingredients at Mahanaga, which serves modern Thai in a funky Moroccan setting. The Summer restaurant offers unusual Thai fusion recipes in a glass house.

While cosmopolitan locals appreciate foreign cuisines, they seldom stray from Thai fare for long. Bangkok restaurants, thus, often combine international food with Thai dishes. Italian food is the most popular Western cuisine here, since its light Mediterranean seafood and noodle dishes, cooked with plenty of garlic, are not so far removed from Thai food. One of the coolest of these restaurants is the Greyhound Café, although Kuppa never seems to fade as the favourite of the city's yuppie crowd.

There's a dizzying array of eateries for Bangkok's young, rich and trendy. These include Thang Long for Vietnamese food in a contemporary Asian chic setting; To Die For's international cuisines in the super-hip H1 complex on Thong Lo Road; and Calderazzo for Italian food. In a mecca for fusion food, C'yan at the Metropolitan leads the way with Mediterranean fusion, and Chi restaurant at the H1 Complex is the choice of the well-heeled young who like Asian fusion. Models and movie stars are also feast for the eyes here.

THIS PAGE (FROM TOP): *Global chic is all the rage in Bangkok bistros; piquant seafood dishes are prominent in Thai cuisine; glitz and chic in a gorgeously kitsch dining environment.*

OPPOSITE (FROM TOP): *The exquisite interior of the Lacquer Pavilion at the Suan Pakkad Palace; Tom Yum Goong has become an international favourite.*

shopping

Shopping is the Thai nation's favourite pastime, second only to eating. After all, it's much more pleasant to spend the weekend buying beautiful new things in a mercifully cool air-conditioned shopping mall than be outside, wilting in the scorching sun! The Thai people's love for shopping spawns a never-ending supply of shopping venues and unique designs. Even neighbouring shopaholics from Singapore and Hong Kong flock here to indulge in bouts of retail madness.

There is an overwhelming variety of shopping options in Bangkok, from luxury malls and exotic night markets, to the mega Chatuchak weekend market. While European luxury brands are always available, the Bangkok shopping scene is known for its high-quality local craftsmanship in furniture, fashion and décor.

For those who love luxury shopping malls, Gaysorn Plaza houses Louis Vuitton, Celine, Prada and Fendi. The recently opened Erawan mall, with shops that include Burberry and Club 21, is just across the street. Emporium mall on Sukhumvit is home to Chanel, Gucci and even more Prada. Other trendy malls for the younger set are Siam Centre and Siam Discovery Centre. On trendy Soi Thonglor, there is the style-oriented H1 complex selling an international lifestyle consisting of European food and Italian designer furniture to Bangkok's cool crowd. Hot on its heels, the new and even trendier

Playground was recently opened just down the street, with a launch party featuring a gargantuan fluorescent pink dinosaur in the atrium. It's a place where rich young things can indulge in the latest offerings of high-style food and fashion.

going out

Bangkok used to be the city that never sleeps, but in recent years the government's Social Order forced night venues to close at 2 am. As if this would stop the Thais from their nocturnal antics. Cool nightclubs still draw the hordes in Bangkok, and most of them embrace the international trends and styles of the moment. The party crowd still shows up at the white-on-white Bed Supperclub; New York lounge-style Q Bar; the swish black and red Met Bar; and the gorgeously streamlined Mystique.

staying in

Boutique hotels are the current trend on the chic Bangkok travel scene. With an emphasis on individuality, exclusivity and glamour, they are always highly accented by design and style. Whether it's a touch of traditional Thai style or an elegant echoing of international design trends, the impeccable hospitality always shines through.

Conrad is proud of its gorgeously turned-out staff, who swish around in neutral-toned silks designed by high-society Thai fashion couturier Pichitra. Meanwhile, The Sukhothai was the first to reveal a modern interpretation of Thai style in its décor and surroundings. Its use of thoughtfully chosen Thai antiquities, Khmer bas-reliefs and sculptures first set the modern-day trend that has since been emulated by many followers. As a place to hang out in style, Chakrabongse Villas offers old-world Thai charm in a colonial-style palace. It is the former residence of Prince Chula Chakrabongse, a half-Russian grandson of Rama V. The riverside property is now owned by his daughter, a publisher of books on Thai culture and the arts. With just three private apartments set in luxuriant gardens, the property provides a popular and elegant venue for private parties, corporate events and launch parties.

THIS PAGE: *Bed Supperclub's space-age interior is the perfect venue for the hottest parties.*

OPPOSITE (FROM TOP): *Bangkok's numerous shopping malls are a mecca for the fashion hungry; cutting-edge local design for both sexes can easily be found.*

fashion city

Next to food, fashion is one of the driving forces of the lifestyle in Bangkok. And it shows. Everywhere you look, people are wearing and consuming fashion. Even the humblest of street vendors sell the latest trends in bags, shoes, accessories and clothes. Indeed, the government's recent pet project—'Bangkok Fashion City'—has a budget of millions to promote Bangkok as the fashion hub of Southeast Asia. High-profile, glamorous events are held to attract top supermodels and fashion designers, creating global awareness of the local fashion industry.

Elle Fashion Week in November is the highlight of Bangkok's fashion scene, with limited tickets that are much coveted by media types, fashion lovers and the city's stylish set. Held in an elegant, air-conditioned tent in the Central Department Store parking lot, it has the air of an international show, similar to the New York Fashion Week shows that are held in custom-built tents in Bryant Park.

The event is an annual showcase for top Thai fashion designers, with the final show always reserved for celebrated fashion doyenne, Nagara, whose gorgeous Oriental glamour concepts never fail to steal the scene.

Other Thai brands are noted for their luxurious silk garments. These include the Thai Silk Company, Paothong's Collection, and Mungdoo, who specialise in making inspiring contemporary interpretations of traditional Asian garments such as Chinese robes, Thai fisherman pants and Bhutanese wrap tops.

Mae Fah Luang is a local textile crafts foundation that promotes traditional cotton woven textiles. It hires talented young textile and fashion designers to create cutting-edge designs for its homegrown cottons.

International acclaim goes to the 10-year-old fashion brand Fly Now, which has opened London Fashion Week twice in recent years, and whose principal designer Chamnam Pakdisuk lives in London. Fly Now's Bangkok boutique is in Gaysorn Plaza. Other top Thai design brands that lead the local fashion scene in international style are Anurak, Greyhound, Soda, Jaspal, Theatre, Tub, and Tango.

THIS PAGE (TOP AND BELOW): *Thai designer Nagara's ab-fab shows are one of the highlights of Bangkok Fashion Week; mega-watt glamour charges the catwalks at the city's high-profile fashion shows.*

TOP RIGHT AND OPPOSITE: *Bangkok's malls are home to all the major European luxury boutiques.*

...fashion is one of the driving forces of the lifestyle in Bangkok.

central plains: fertile plains, artistic kingdoms

The lush central plains of Thailand are known for their thriving agricultural riches. This is where Sukhothai and Ayutthaya lie, the country's glorious historical capitals which stood before the present capital of Bangkok was founded. These two ancient kingdoms were renowned for their prosperity, and the arts and culture that flourished during their heyday eras laid the foundation for the arts and design that became typical Thai style.

What made the arts flourish so much in these cities? This region is the most fertile part of a fertile country. The land here is fed by the Chao Phraya river and a network of canals, and sees plenty of rain. It enjoys the abundance from the richest crops of rice, fruits, and fish in the rivers. Because of the plentiful supply of food, the living was good. Civilisation and the arts flourished because the inhabitants were content, and their lifestyle was all about the celebration of living and beauty. No wonder the arts reached such glorious heights in these cities.

sukhothai history: the dawn of happiness

The kingdom of Sukhothai reflected Thailand's golden era. Founded long ago in the 13th century, it was the first real unified Thai kingdom, then known as Siam. Previously, the communities consisted of many city states around Chiang Mai and the Khmer empire. The new kingdom of Sukhothai stretched in all directions from its capital city and included Pitsanoulok in the east, Si Satchanalai in the north, Kamphaeng Phet in the west and Nakorn Sawan in the south. Sukhothai means 'Dawn of Happiness' in Sanskrit, which celebrates the kingdom's enjoyment of peace and prosperity. Although the Sukhothai era lasted only two centuries, its influence is still felt in Thai culture today. The kingdom's greatest ruler was its third monarch, King Ramkhamhaeng. During his reign, Thai Theravada Buddhism was codified, the Thai alphabet came into being, and stunning works of art and sculpture were created. The kingdom became involved in active trade with other countries, and prospered especially in exporting ceramics to China. More than 400 kilns were producing distinctively Thai glazed ceramics known

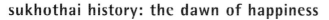

THIS PAGE: *The ancient ruins of Sukhothai glittering during the Loy Krathong Festival is a magical experience.*

OPPOSITE: *Even stone sculptures like this giant reclining Buddha seem to succumb to the dreamy serenity of romantic Ayutthaya.*

as celadon, ready for export. Many of these kilns are deemed archaeological sites today and still turn up pieces of ancient pottery.

Sukhothai was absorbed by the kingdom of Ayutthaya in the 15th century. Today it is a UNESCO World Heritage Site, which includes a neighbouring site at Si Satchanalai-Chaliang, and is 50 km (31 miles) north of Sukhothai.

sightseeing: ruins

The majesty and beauty of the city ruins still embody an aura of grace and tranquillity that even today gives you an inkling of how elegant the original must have been. Towering Buddha figures emerge from the pillars and stones of ancient temples. A Sukhothai Buddha seated in tranquil meditation above the stillness of a mist-shrouded lotus pond at dawn is one of the unforgettable images of classic Thailand.

The ancient city is now contained in what is known as Sukhothai Historical Park and consists of 21 sites within a 5-km (3-mile) radius.

The abundance of temples indicates it was a society devoted to religion, and the important building was the temple at the centre of the community. Among the many temples that highlight the Sukhothai ruins, several are outstanding in beauty and cultural significance. Wat Mahathat is the largest temple in the city. It dates back from the 13th century, and has a giant seated Buddha figure surrounded by the remains of the pillars that used to support the temple building. The temple is sheltered by a brick wall and a moat, which represent the outer wall of the universe and the cosmic ocean. One of the most photogenic sites is Wat Si Chum, where a towering seated Buddha nestles within a shrine hall. Its imposing size is impressive but it is the statue's exquisite serenity of expression and its gentle smile that proves awe-inspiring. This perfectly balanced face is a stunning example of Sukhothai style. Another temple of astonishing beauty is Wat Sa Si, or Sacred Pond Temple. Located on an island in the middle of a lotus pond with a large Buddha figure rising from among the ruins of pillars, the temple's memorable image has been captured on thousands of postcards of Thailand.

artistic traditions

Religion played an important role in Sukhothai society, but the religious architecture of the time was relatively understated, compared to the glittering grandeur of the eras that followed. While there was a visible evolution of architectural styles over the two Sukhothai centuries, there are distinct features that characterise the era as a whole.

From the designs of the religious buildings it is clear that the kingdom was a Hindu-Buddhist society, but that Buddhism was the dominant religion. Khmer influences can be seen in the Hindu prangs (rounded towers) of the earlier 13th-century buildings.

And the Sri Lankan style—a type of temple architecture brought back from Sri Lanka by a later Sukhothai prince—is evident in the Sinhalese-style bell-shaped stupas around the city. Stupas with lotus-bud tops are pure Sukhothai, as are the tall, narrow halls built to house massive standing Buddha figures. Temples surrounded by brick walls and moats, symbolising Hindu cosmology, are also the classic hallmarks of Sukhothai religious architecture.

Seated Buddhas with a high flame finial also originated in the Sukhothai period and this style is visibly prevalent around the ruins, too. Like the Western halo, the flame symbolises spiritual radiance and enlightenment. The Sukhothai walking Buddha marks a stylistic change in sculpture from the Khmer style before it, which was characterised by chunky figures with thick-set heavy facial features, full lips and square faces.

The elegant Sukhothai Buddha figures exemplified a new, completely Thai identity marked by rounded features and sensuous lines. The face became oval with a soft, rounded chin, downcast eyes and arched eyebrows, while the body looks smooth and sinuous, devoid of the corporeal fleshiness of a real human body.

THIS PAGE: *These elongated fingers tapering into sinuous curves are characteristic of the elegant style of Sukhothai Buddha figures.*
OPPOSITE: *Sukhothai abounds with scenes of simple yet powerful beauty, like these tranquil temple ruins hauntingly reflected in a lotus pond.*

Sukhothai and neighbouring town Si Satchanalai were renowned for producing glazed ceramics, especially celadon. The ceramics were mostly produced in kilns in a town called Sawankhalok, and the pottery came to be known as Sangkalok or Si Satchanalai pottery. These ceramics are distinguished by their brown, two-colour glazed decorative figurines or vessels in human and animal shapes. Distinctive ceramic motifs were the fish, lotus, and floral patterns, found on many plates and bowls of that period.

ayutthaya history: a glittering kingdom

The gold embellishments and intricate design motifs that came to embody classic Thai style reached their apex in the glittering Ayutthaya period, the most magnificent kingdom in Thai history. The Ayutthaya kingdom was so prosperous and its court so magnificent that it was the envy of its neighbours, and was held in awe by the many foreigners who traded with it. Founded in 1350, and named after the mythical city of Ayodhya, the home of Rama in the Indian epic the *Ramayana*, it was the royal capital of Siam until 1767 when it was conquered and destroyed by the Burmese.

The Ayutthaya period lasted over 400 years and at its height, the kingdom stretched into what are now Laos, Cambodia and Myanmar. By the 17th century it boasted over one million inhabitants—greater than the population of London at the time. As a thriving commercial trading port, it was one of the wealthiest cities in Asia, and hosted an international community of Portuguese, Dutch, English, French, Chinese and Japanese merchants and missionaries.

The Thai word for foreigner, farang, originated from this period—a derivation of 'farangsais' for French people. The cosmopolitan kingdom was open to change and absorbed many foreign influences into its culture.

Highly tolerant of foreigners was King Narai, one of the great Ayutthaya kings. During his reign, a Greek named Constantine Phaulkon served as prime minister, from 1675 to 1688. He was friendly with the French but kept Dutch and English people out. Eventually the Thais became nervous of him, executed him and expelled the French. They did not welcome Westerners into the country for the next 150 years.

The kingdom's wealth was a source of great envy to the Burmese. They launched a series of invasions and conquered the city in 1767, destroying temples and palaces, and many artworks, manuscripts and sculptures. But, the Burmese did not stay in power and the Thais reunited under Taksin.

ayutthaya: temple ruins

The number of temple ruins scattered across the historical site illustrates the scope of the capital. The largest temple site is Wat Phra Si Sanphet, which was once a royal palace. Built in the 14th century, it housed a 16 m (52 ft) standing Buddha covered in gold, which was melted down when the Burmese ransacked the city. Its three romantic-looking stupas have become the symbol of Ayutthaya.

THIS PAGE: *Saffron-robed monks descend from a temple ruin.*

OPPOSITE (FROM TOP): *View of Ayutthaya from above; the Walking Buddha, like this one at Wat Mahathat Chalieng in Si Satchanalai, is a distinctive Thai sculptural motif.*

Another famous 14th-century temple in Ayutthaya is Wat Phra Mahathat, with its massive prang (Khmer-style tower). Although much of it was destroyed by the Burmese, one of its most magical features is a stone Buddha head, wrapped in the loving roots of a Banyan tree in the temple grounds. With a sweet smile, it has the appearance of enjoying a divine slumber in the generous protection of the Banyan tree.

While much of the city was left in charred ruins by the invading Burmese, a rare example of a temple that escaped destruction is Wat Na Phra Meru. Its walls, pillars and beautiful carved wooden ceiling remain intact, and nestled inside is a an Ayutthaya-style seated Buddha, 6 m (20 ft) high and wearing a glorious crown.

artistic traditions

The stupas (or chedis) of Ayutthaya display the evolution of many shapes over the period. The earlier ones have the Khmer-influenced prang shape, as seen at Wat Sorn and Wat Phutthaisawan. Another type is the Sinhalese bell-shaped stupa that became popular when Sri Lankan Buddhism flourished in the 15th century. These stupas were decorated with animals like lions and garudas—creatures of Buddhist mythology.

The wealth and magnificence of the kingdom is reflected in its luxurious 16th- and 18th-century Buddha figures. The proud monarchs, who were patrons of religion and the arts, commissioned Buddha images to wear crowns and royal regalia embellished with sparkling jewels. Mimicking the court dress of the period, the Buddhas' garments are jewelled and elaborately decorated with floral patterns, a contrast to the austere simplicity of the preceding Sukhothai Buddhas. They are often shown standing or else seated on tiered jewelled thrones.

Thai mural painting was also important during this period, although much of the artwork was destroyed by invaders. Ayutthaya painting was known for its elegant murals depicting the life of Buddha. Other paintings of the era portray secular scenes of an opulent royal court with kings and courtiers, resplendent in fabulous jewels, crowns, headdresses and gorgeous garments.

THIS PAGE (FROM TOP): Monks at their daily tasks are a timeless sight in Ayutthaya's many temples; this Buddha head appears in blissfully slumber wrapped in the loving embrace of a Banyan tree at Wat Phra Mahathat.

OPPOSITE: Barges and stilt houses along the waterways are an enduring feature of Thailand's countryside.

With a sweet smile, it has the appearance of enjoying a divine slumber...

northeast: the thai heartland

Thailand's northeast region, bordered by Laos and Cambodia, is known as Isan. It is considered the real heartland of Thailand. Consisting of 19 rural farm provinces, it is less fertile than the plains of central Thailand, and as a result many Isan natives migrate to the capital and other cities seeking better economic opportunities. Most of the country's taxi drivers, maids and waiters come from this region of Thailand.

A high percentage of Thailand's upwardly mobile, middle-class urban population is of Chinese ethnic origin—people who were immigrants a few generations ago. The people of Isan, however, are considered the true ethnic Thai people—their origins are rooted in the farmland of a predominantly agrarian society. The Isan region has Laotian and Cambodian cultural influences, and the dialect is much closer to Lao than Thai.

Isan has its own style of music, mostly derived from local wind instruments made of bamboo. The khaen is played like a mouth organ and produces the distinctive sound of Thai folk music. The northeast also has its own style of pop music, called luuk thung, meaning 'child of the fields.' It is infectiously upbeat and featured on its very own radio station—a favourite of taxi drivers around Thailand. The songs are about love and hardship, reflecting the lives of Isan people who struggle with poverty and grief but retain their sense of humour and friendly outlook.

Isan was once part of the glorious Khmer empire. It was here that one of Asia's oldest civilisations flourished, so the region is now archaeology territory. Near the Laotian border lies the archaeological site of Ban Chiang, a 4,000-year old bronze culture known for its pottery and metallurgy. A new national museum at the site displays the many bronze and pottery artefacts from the era. Ban Chiang pottery is identified by its orange-coloured pots and vessels, decorated with a dark orange swirl motif that appears surprisingly contemporary in its simplicity. The site was declared a UNESCO World Heritage site in 1992. Compared to the rest of the country's great abundance, Isan is known as Thailand's poorest region. Yet with its food, music and traditional handicrafts, it still makes a key contribution to Thai culture and style.

THIS PAGE (FROM TOP): *The khaen is a mouth organ that produces the distinctive and popular sound of Thai country music; the parched remains of an ancient civilisation were found in Ban Chiang in the northeast.* OPPOSITE: *A solitary water buffalo greets the new day in Thailand's rural northeast.*

ancient heritage

Because the northeast region of Thailand was part of the mighty Khmer empire, there are numerous intriguing archaeological ruins around the Cambodian-border area of Isan. Although some of the ruins are from the magnificent Angkor period of Khmer history, most pre-date it. The majority of the ruins are located in four provinces: Buriram, Nakhon Ratchasima, Surin and Si Sakhet. The largest ruins are called prasat in Thai, referring to large temple sanctuaries. They are famous for their bas-relief carvings, which were adopted centuries later as contemporary décor features in hotels. When Bangkok's stylish Sukhothai, for example, used Khmer-style bas-reliefs in its lobby, it effectively set the trend for other hotels, restaurants and private homes to follow. Reproduction Khmer bas-reliefs are popular items in antiques and décor shops, too, often sold as contemporary decorations for the interiors and gardens of people's homes. In fact, the taste for Khmer sculpture has become so popular in recent times that is has spawned innovative Khmer-inspired gifts and household wares. Scented candles depicting scenes from intricate bas-reliefs, for example, are snapped up by trendy home owners in Bangkok's décor shops.

Khmer ruins are Hindu, which was the religion of the Khmer culture. The carvings depict the Hindu deities Vishnu and Shiva, instead of the Buddhist iconography that symbolises Thai style. And Phanom Rung Historical Park is the largest and best restored of all the Khmer ruins in Thailand. Its name means 'big hill' in Khmer but in Thai it is called Prasat Hin Khao Phanom Rung, which translates as 'Stone Temple on Phanom Rung Hill.' The temple complex is indeed on top of a hill, or rather an extinct volcano peak easily visible for miles in the otherwise flat Isan countryside. It lies just south of the main Isan towns of Khorat, Buriram and Surin, and from the top you can see the Dongrek mountains of Cambodia to the east. The complex faces this direction, which is also the direction of Angkor Wat, the Khmer capital. The eastward orientation means it also faces the dawn—typical of Hindu temple architecture. Built during the reign of King Suriyavarman II, which was considered the height of Angkor architecture, Phanom

Rung is the best surviving example of Khmer style in Thailand. As a Hindu monument, it has a beautiful, long promenade leading from the front gate to the temple building.

Phanom Rung sculptures exemplify a quality of craftsmanship comparable to the sophisticated reliefs of Angkor Wat in Cambodia. The site is renowned for its well-carved lintels, with the famous Phra Narai lintel the source of great controversy in the arts world for some years. It mysteriously disappeared in the early 1960s, eventually turning up at the Art Institute of Chicago as a donation by an American named James Alsdorf. The Thai government spent years trying to recover it and the lintel was finally returned to its original home in 1988 by the Alsdorf foundation, in exchange for

THIS PAGE: *Imposing Phanom Rung is the largest and best example of Khmer-style architecture.*

OPPOSITE (FROM TOP): *Beads and amulets excavated from the 4,000-year-old Ban Chiang site in northeastern Thailand; this statue of King Jayavarma VII in a temple in Phimai shows the solid features, thick lips and square face so typical of the Khmer style.*

US$250,000 and an arrangement for regular loans of Thai artifacts to the Art Insitute of Chicago.

One of the best-known Khmer ruins is the hauntingly beautiful Prasat Hin Phimai National Historical Park. Built in the 10th to 11th centuries, the Hindu Buddhist temple is easily distinguished by a shrine made of white sandstone, with surrounding shrines made from pink sandstone and laterite. Its numerous sculptures remain well preserved. Nearby is the Phimai National Museum, displaying many examples of the outstanding Khmer sculptures in Thailand.

An added attraction when visiting Phimai is the country's oldest and largest Banyan tree—so large that it spreads over an island in a large pond, with walkways through the branches.

One of the most dramatic of the Angkor period sites in Isan is Khao Phra Viharn in the Si Sakhet province. Located on the Thai-Cambodian border, it actually belongs to Cambodia in terms of geography, although the two countries wrestled for territorial claims over the site for many years. Ironically, Khao Phra Viharn is inaccessible from the Cambodian side and visitors must pass a Thai army checkpoint and leave photographic ID to enter.

The temple complex was built during the 10th to 12th centuries under a succession of Khmer kings. It sits on the edge of a 600 m (1,969 ft) cliff, offering a dramatic panorama of the pristine Cambodian landscape on the other side. Although the site suffered some pillaging of artefacts during the Khmer Rouge occupation, many of the temple's stone carvings are still intact and the complex is partially restored, giving you more than just a hint of its past beauty.

THIS PAGE: The stately ruins at Phimai show the Khmer-style influence on the temple prangs.

OPPOSITE (FROM TOP): Country fare, with a container of sticky rice; Somtam, or papaya pok pok, the spicy Thai salad; juicy grilled pork neck dipped in spicy chilli sauce is a classically Isan favourite.

country fare

Of the country's regional cuisines, Isan food is one of the most distinctive. To Thai people, this is real Thai food. It's the food of the country people, quite unlike the subtler dishes of the cities, and loved for its strong flavours and liberal use of fresh chillies and garlic. The most famous Isan dish is the spicy green papaya salad, known as Somtam or Papaya Pok-Pok—a nickname echoing the rhythmic thumping of the mortar and pestle used to prepare it. Shredded fresh green papaya with green beans, tomatoes, garlic, fish sauce, limes, chillies, and a touch of palm sugar are pounded together to blend the flavours.

Somtam Puu is a popular version using freshwater crab for added piquancy. And trendy Bangkok restaurants serve up shrimp or seafood Somtam versions, with delicate flavours that taste more refined.

The papaya salad is eaten with juicy charcoal-grilled chicken and sticky rice—the northeastern staple alternative to the soft-boiled rice found in Central Thailand. It is steamed in a basket and eaten with the hands by rolling the chewy rice into a little ball and dipping it in sauce.

Grilled pork neck, or Khaw Moo Yang, and a spicy, sour chicken or pork salad made with fresh limes and chillies, or larb, are other Isan favourites. Isan dishes tend to be spicy and are served with vegetables and a zesty dipping sauce made of fish sauce, chillies and tamarind. If you like your food with an extra kick, ask for it served up "zaap zaap"—the Isan slang tastes exactly how it sounds!

As with any country fare, the region has its own style of sausage. The Isan sausage is thick and fermented, grilled on a stick until crisp and juicy, and eaten with crunchy fresh cabbage, green beans and fresh ginger. Another type of northeastern sausage is called Nam, a raw version made of pickled pork and pork rinds. Fermented in banana leaf, nam has a sharp, sour taste. It is eaten with fresh ginger, chillies and peanuts like a snack, and is also popular served up as nam-fried rice.

textiles and handicrafts

Beautiful silks come from Isan, where hand-woven textiles are the regional speciality. In 2004 it was the location of a glamorous Thai silk festival, hosted by the Thai government and attended by jetset Italian couturier Valentino. Pak Thong Chai is a good place to buy silk and observe silk-weaving practices, while Khon Kaen is also great for purchasing silk, cotton and traditional basketware.

The region is known for its traditional cotton fabrics, too, especially Thai mudmee, which resembles Indonesian ikat weaves. Another favourite is the triangular pillow called mawn kwaan, or axe pillow. Now a highly familiar item of contemporary Thai décor, mawn kwaan traditionally provided back support for people who spent most of their time seated on cool wooden floors or reed mats.

festivals: elephant fantasia

Of the brightly coloured festivals hosted by Isan every year—including the masked Phii Takon Festival and the exciting Yasothon Rocket Festival—the most memorable is the Surin Elephant Festival. Normally a sleepy provincial town, Surin thunders into action every November with this magical event. The festival originated from the traditional annual elephant round-up, when wild elephants were captured and tamed for domestic work like logging and construction. Nowadays, elephants of all sizes are brought from around the country to perform in a festival show, delighting audiences with clever tricks, elaborate re-enactments of historical battle scenes, and elephant soccer. There are many opportunities for animal feeding in the parade grounds after the show, and children delight in riding baby elephants bareback around the field. There are souvenirs everywhere, all bearing images of Thailand's best-loved creature.

But the highlight of the festival must surely be the dozens of elephants roaming the streets offering rides to pedestrians. Taking an elephant taxi from your hotel is a de rigueur part of the festivities, and there are so many of them on parade that you can choose the size that suits you best, from XXL to... jumbo.

THIS PAGE (FROM TOP): Fun elephant football is a highlight at the Surin Elephant Festival; the northeast is known for its weaving industry, where Thai silk is made by hand.
OPPOSITE: Gaudily painted masks symbolise frolicking spirits at the annual Phii Takon Festival.

Normally a sleepy provincial town, Surin thunders into action every November...

The Baan Thai Wellness Retreat

Before the current ubiquitous concrete houses and tall apartment buildings began appearing in Bangkok several decades ago, Thailand's capital city was rich with traditional teak homes, complete with ornate Oriental rooftops in beautiful bright colours. Such traditional Thai architecture is hard to find now in the city, much less a historical family home that has retained its original design from generations past.

This is precisely what makes the The Baan Thai Wellness Retreat so precious. Built more than 60 years ago by M. R. Bongsebrahma, a grandson of Rama IV, this traditional Thai teak house has remained in the family since it was built. In 1965, the family decided to share its heritage with the public by turning Baan Thai into a restaurant, which served fine Thai cuisine while entertaining guests with authentic Thai dance performances. Baan Thai drew celebrities from all over the world including Tiger Woods, Jackie Kennedy and Japanese royalty.

Today, Baan Thai has once again been restored through renovations in the original

THIS PAGE (FROM TOP): Baan Sombhan features an oversized bathtub; traditional Thai teak and ornate roofs are a signature of Baan Thai Heritage Home.

OPPOSITE: Original antiques and objects decorate rich teak spaces, like the bedroom suite.

...this traditional Thai teak house has been with the family since it was built.

buildings, and the addition of several traditional teak wood houses from Ayutthaya. Instead of offering sumptuous, classic Thai food, however, Baan Thai now offers a taste of old-world Thailand by serving as a luxurious wellness retreat.

Though retaining original structures, the homes have been fitted with modern luxuries like exquisitely designed bathrooms and air-conditioning. The décor is a mix of contemporary and traditional, with teakwood furnishings and fine Thai artefacts that once belonged to the family.

Now a collection of several houses, Baan Thai boasts private and shared swimming pools, and exclusive tropical gardens. Each house has its own unique character. Baan Dossiriwongse, for example, has a sweeping original roof structure, which affords wonderfully high ceilings. Baan Sombhan features a multi-level interior with ensuite bathrooms fitted with an oversized bathtub and enclosed shower. Baan Wanwaew's traditional Thai sala is the perfect place to curl up to a good book or enjoy a traditional Thai massage.

Indulge in luxurious spa treatments inspired by sister property Phu Chai Sai Resort and Spa. Or enjoy a cooking class. You will wish you could stay forever.

PHOTOGRAPHS COURTESY OF BAAN THAI HERITAGE HOME.

FACTS	
ROOMS	12 suites • 10 rooms
FOOD	Restaurant: Thai spa
DRINK	Juice and Elixir Bar
FEATURES	spa • pool • library • fitness centre • yoga • meditation • cooking classes • flower arranging classes
NEARBY	Thonglor and Phromphong stations • Emporium Shopping Complex • Benjasiri National Park
CONTACT	7 Soi Sukhumvit 32, Sukhumvit Road, Klongton, Klongtoey, Bangkok 10110 • telephone: +66.2.258 5403 • facsimile: +66.2.258 9517 • email: contact@thebaanthai.com • website: www.thebaanthai.com

Conrad Bangkok

Wireless Road is Bangkok's most sought-after business address, and the All Season's Place Complex is its most cutting-edge office, retail, residential and hotel development. It is only natural then, that the hotel name on everyone's lips is right at the heart of it all.

Conrad Bangkok, from the Conrad Hotels group, is already well known as the city's funkiest business hotel. It's an oxymoron of a description but Conrad Bangkok balances classic sophistication with cutting-edge concepts. So if you're expecting a traditional approach to Thai style, you'll be pleasantly surprised. Conrad Bangkok complements the best of its host city's ancient and elegant elements with contemporary yet thoughtful precision.

Think of the hotel as an elegant office block skilfully blending corporate chic with luxurious suites. Rooms are large, open-concept spaces, tastefully yet fashionably furnished, and equipped with every modern convenience: high-speed broadband Internet access, laptop/facsimilie/printer set-ups and a universal pin plug socket. The Executive Floor rooms have it all, too: from private check-in to a well-equipped business centre, meeting rooms, and a relaxing Executive Floor Lounge. It comes as no surprise that *Business Traveller* magazine rated Conrad Bangkok the 'Best Business

...an office block skilfully blending corporate chic with undisputedly luxurious suites.

Hotel in Asia-Pacific' for two consecutive years. It also won 'Thailand's Leading Business Hotel' in the Annual World Travel Awards 2005, and deservedly so.

Once your working day is done, take a break on the rooftop jogging track, a dip in ozone-treated swimming pool or a pampering session in the spa. Ask for the indulgent pillow menu upon check-in to ensure your blissful slumber. It has everything from grass to natural rubber to ensure you drift off to an energising sleep. While word spreads about Conrad Bangkok's state-of-the-art rooms and facilities, it is the hotel's ritzy dining and drinking scene that attracts the most fashionable circles. Liu, another visionary concept by Zhang Jin Jie of Beijing's Green T House fame, brings a Chinese gourmet revolution to Bangkok in both culinary and decorative styles. The dark shutters and jazz of the Diplomat Bar host Bangkok's chic pre- and post-dinner set, while the 87 Plus club is graced by the creative, socialite and business crowd. Indeed, the working trip has never been this pleasurable.

THIS PAGE (FROM LEFT): Enjoy jazz at the rich-hued Diplomat Bar; decorated in soft, warm tones, all 392 rooms feature every modern comfort.

OPPOSITE: Like massive tree trunks or oversized bamboo, the columns in the lobby tower over the welcoming sofas and natural floors.

FACTS		
ROOMS	34 suites • 358 executive, deluxe and classic rooms	
FOOD	Liu: Chinese • Italianate: Italian •Drinking Tea Eating Rice: Japanese • City Terrace: poolside • Café@2: international • Deli by Conrad: bakery	
DRINK	Diplomat Bar • 87 Plus: nightclub	
FEATURES	Seasons Spa • Bodyworx fitness centre	
NEARBY	Lumpini Park • Skytrain • Siam Square • Queen Sirikit Convention Centre	
CONTACT	87 Wireless Road, Bangkok 10330 • telephone: +66.2.690 9999 • facsimile: +66.2.690 9000 • email: info@conradbangkok.com • website: www.conradhotels.com	

PHOTOGRAPHS COURTESY OF CONRAD BANGKOK.

The Dusit Thani, Bangkok

Located in the heart of Bangkok's business, shopping and entertainment district, The Dusit Thani, Bangkok has made a name for itself as one of the city's finest hotels. Amongst its 517 luxuriously appointed guest rooms are its unique Thai Heritage Suites that bear distinctive decorative motifs from this rich culture. State-of-the-art business and fitness facilities, as well as the essential amenities, make your time here a pleasure. Complementing these, the hotel boasts fine food and beverage outlets to suit the most demanding of tastes.

The jewel in Dusit Thani's culinary crown is its French fine dining restaurant D'Sens. This remarkable restaurant was modelled on the famous Le Jardin des Sens in Montpellier, France—one of only 27 restaurants in France to be awarded three prestigious Michelin stars. D'Sens was created by twin brothers Jacques and Laurent Pourcel, hailed by gourmands around the globe as two of the world's finest chefs. Influenced by their home province of Languedoc in southern France, the brothers have produced a menu combining Mediterranean-style cooking with carefully

The jewel in Dusit Thani's culinary crown is its French fine dining restaurant D'Sens.

selected Thai ingredients. The result is a truly memorable dining experience redolent with exciting tastes and dramatic flavours. Unsurprisingly, gastronomes have been flocking to D'Sens since it opened in 2004.

Insurpassable cuisine demands divine décor: at D'Sens, the interiors were created by international designer, Imaad Rhamouni. Pass through a spectacular curtain of handcrafted glass beads before being guided to a private booth, decked with leather banquettes and chairs, posed on Paul Smith carpets. Admire huge aquariums full of tropical fish or the breathtaking views of the city and Lumpini Park below.

After dinner, enjoy drinks at Dusit Thani's MyBar—a wild mix of modern décor with illuminated white glass and polished metal trims. Sit back in MyBar's plush lounge and lap up live jazz from the resident band. When the band takes a break and the DJ appears, groove to R&B and pop tunes before calling it a (fabulous) night.

PHOTOGRAPHS COURTESY OF THE DUSIT THANI, BANGKOK.

FACTS

ROOMS	29 suites • 488 rooms
FOOD	D'Sens: New French • Il Cielo: Italian • Hamilton's Steak House: American • Benjarong: Royal Thai • Thien Duong: Vietnamese • The Mayflower: Cantonese • Shogun: Japanese • The Pavilion: international • Dusit Gourmet: cakes and pastries
DRINK	MyBar • Lobby Lounge • ChampagneS lounge
FEATURES	spa • sauna • fitness centre • pool • Internet access • shops • business centre
NEARBY	shopping centres • railway station • Lumpini Park • business district
CONTACT	946 Rama IV Road, Bangkok 10500 • telephone: +66.22.009 000 • facsimile: +66.22.366 400 • email: dusitbkk@dusit.com • website: www.dusit.com

Emporium Suites

They don't call the Emporium Suites the ultimate serviced residence for nothing. Its arresting presence in the heart of Bangkok's main Sukhumvit thoroughfare is the first sign of the plush grandeur that is accorded to all its residents. Step through its glass doors and a warm reception staff greets you, just like in a five-star hotel, except here, you can stay for a week, months or years—it is a place, after all, that many call home. Its décor is inviting and understated; hip yet elegant. Scarlet egg chairs dot the reception and lobby lounge against a backdrop of deep chocolate carpets and soft biscuit settees. In all its spacious suites, this warm décor carries through, with dark wood furnishings, rich olive carpets and cream accents that lift the ambience from modern contemporary to of-the-moment chic.

There are a total of 378 suites, ranging in size from 65 sq m (670 sq ft) to a sprawling 515 sq m (5,543 sq ft) four-bedroom penthouse. In one-, two- or three-

THIS PAGE (FROM TOP): Breakfast by the pool surrounded by greenery; the lush landscape continues through the gym exterior; suites are tastefully accented with earth tones and rich carpets.

OPPOSITE: Suites range in size up to the four-bedroom penthouse; the stylish Emporia Restaurant.

...these luxurious suites command panoramic city views.

bedroom configurations, these luxurious suites command panoramic city views. They are equipped with all the modern conveniences that have come to be expected of any serviced residence worth its pricey designer chairs—high-speed Internet access, satellite TV, DVD player, stereo hi-fi and IDD telephone line. Even its kitchens are superbly furnished and equipped —built-in ovens and microwaves are elegantly streamlined with brushed metal finishes.

Within the building is a range of facilities that would make any luxury hotel proud. A charming children's playground could keep little tykes busy for hours, while a free-form swimming pool and jacuzzi allows adults to unwind in its liquid comforts. A state-of-the-art fitness centre lets residents do away with their external gym memberships, while a sauna and steam room helps to work up a sweat without the treadmill. For exquisite

pampering, the Clarins spa by Sense and Spirit is also on-site should residents feel like a much-needed massage.

Right downstairs sits the fashionable Emporium Shopping Complex, Bangkok's exciting premier shopping, dining and entertainment venue. Schools, embassies, hospitals and office buildings are all within easy reach. Indeed, the Emporium Suites are the ultimate home away from home experience for the discerning individual.

FACTS

ROOMS	378 suites
FOOD	The Emporia Restaurant: Cantonese • Japanese • Thai • European • room service
DRINK	lobby lounge • poolside terrace/bar
FEATURES	business centre • conference and function rooms • children's playground • spa • sauna • steam room • limousine service • outdoor swimming pool • jacuzzi • gym • daily newspaper and breakfast
NEARBY	BTS Skytrain • Emporium Shopping Complex • Benjasiri Park
CONTACT	622 Sukhumvit Road, Klongton, Klongtoey, Bangkok 10110 • telephone: +66.2.664 9999 • facsimile: +66.2.664 9990 • email: info@emporiumsuites.com • website: www.emporiumsuites.com

Four Seasons Hotel Bangkok

In 1982, as Bangkok celebrated its bicentennial, a hotel was designed and built as a meeting place of two worlds: one of efficiency and practicality, and the other of Thai graciousness and tradition. The layout of the hotel was based on a typical Thai home and features two atriums or courtyards connected to its main area. Corridors and room entryways face a huge tropical garden that offers serenity and respite.

Almost a decade later, this grand architectural landmark is now known as Four Seasons Hotel Bangkok. Over the last few years, it has been refurbished and restored to perhaps even greater grandeur, and has consistently won awards and accolades for its hospitality, design and service.

Located on Rajadamri Road—one of the city's most famous boulevards—the hotel

features 340 superbly decorated rooms, including 24 suites and eight unique Garden cabanas. These are luxurious environments that reflect the design philosophies of this urban resort. Thai silks, cotton and sumptuous chenille fabrics pay homage to its Thai heritage, accented by a colour scheme of powder red, gold and celadon green. All the rooms at Four Seasons Hotel Bangkok are amongst the

Thai silks, cotton and sumptuous chenille fabrics pay homage to its Thai heritage...

delicious Thai Restaurant in Bangkok". Good food complements excellent design, with bottles of Thai spices lining the restaurant's teak shelves, and gunnysacks of rice and salt sitting on ledges around the room.

Enjoy the hotel's other dining outlets as well: Biscotti, an Italian restaurant; Madison, contemporary American steakhouse; and Shintaro, which serves innovative Japanese cuisine. All are designed by award-winning Tony Chi, and draw a regular crowd, both day and night.

Discerning shoppers can take their pick of premier stores at the Parichart Shopping Arcade. You'll find the best Thai silks, arts, crafts and gems, as well as salons and tailors. And if you need a massage to soothe aching muscles, the hotel's Health Club (incidentally one of Bangkok's most stylish) boasts treatments like Thai and Oriental massages. Indeed, there is something for everyone at this Thai legend.

largest in the city and they are further graced by tasteful marble bathrooms and modern amenities to meet your every need.

Dining is also a major part of this grand hotel. Its Thai restaurant, The Spice Market, has been voted by locals as the "most

THIS PAGE (FROM LEFT): Both the delectable Thai cuisine and design of restaurant space impress at The Spice Market; the Parichart Court offers a lush respite from the city outside.

OPPOSITE: A suite living room embraces chic decadence and Thai heritage.

FACTS	**ROOMS**	24 suites • 8 cabanas • 308 rooms
	FOOD	Biscotti: Italian • Spice Market: Thai • Shintaro: Japanese • The Lobby: snacks • The Terrace: Italian/snacks • Aqua: snacks • Madison: steakhouse
	DRINK	Aqua • The Lobby • The Terrace
	FEATURES	Mandara Spa • health club • banquet facilities • boutique • limousines • business centre • executive club
	NEARBY	Royal Bangkok Sports Club
	CONTACT	155 Rajadamri Road, Bangkok 10330 • telephone: +66.2.250.1000 • facsimile: +66.2.254.5391 • email: reservations.bangkok@fourseasons.com • website: www.fourseasons.com/bangkok

The Mayfair Marriott Executive Apartments

The Marriott name has been considered synonymous with great hospitality for decades. With five-star hotels in most major international cities, the Marriott certainly knows how to pamper its guests with world-class facilities and luxurious comforts.

Naturally, to cater for business travellers whose work takes them away from home for lengthy periods, the Marriott created its signature Executive Apartments. Much like the Marriott hotels, these apartments afford the ideal combination of home-style living with all the indulgences of hotel services.

THIS PAGE (FROM TOP): *Fresh flowers and a cosy rug show the Marriott's attention to detail; the gorgeous pool with awe-inspiring views over Bangkok.*

OPPOSITE (FROM LEFT): *Regal reds and golds feature in the bedrooms' décor; the airy living area is perfect for savouring a coffee and enjoying a relaxing read.*

The Mayfair Marriott in the heart of Bangkok is no different. Situated in the central business district, and close to the main embassies, the Mayfair Marriott offers extended-stay travellers a plush base away from home. Just minutes away are the city's major department stores, excellent Thai, Asian and international restaurants, as well as Skytrain stations. Step out of the property's doors and you'll be greeted by the greenery of Lumpini, Bangkok's biggest park. With a serene lake, jogging trails and plenty of well-tended gardens, Lumpini provides an oasis of nature, away from Bangkok's busy urban life.

Inside the apartments, the furnishings are just as comfortable as they are elegant. A gourmet kitchen complements your

...a plush base away from home.

exploring Bangkok's unbeatable sights is easy. The Marriott Mayfair can arrange tours of the city's most revered temples, its floating markets, rose gardens, and even crocodile wrestling and elephant shows. Indeed, all the excellent services of a five-star hotel can be expected at Marriott Mayfair Executive Apartments. The only difference is that guests call these stellar apartments 'home'.

culinary skills, but if you lack in that department, the Bistro lounge or the new Pool Bar offer a delicious alternative.

There is a total of 162 residences, in one-, two- or three-bedroom configurations. Spacious and sophisticated, they all measure a minimum of 54 sq m (581 sq ft) and go up to 186 sq m (2,002 sq ft) of luxurious living space. Each has the full

complement of hotel-style services—laundry, grocery delivery, room service, minimum twice-weekly housekeeping, concierge and business services.

To unwind or add a spot of activity to the working day, a large swimming pool, sauna, jacuzzi and state-of-the-art gym on the 25th floor offer stunning views of the magnificent city below. And on weekends,

FACTS		
	ROOMS	162 apartments
	FOOD	Bistro Lounge: international • Pool Bar: international • room service: international
	DRINK	Bistro Lounge • Pool Bar • room service
	FEATURES	spa • fitness centre • pool • jacuzzi
	NEARBY	Lumpini Park • embassies • central business district • shopping
	CONTACT	60 Soi Langsuan, Lumpini, Pathumwan, Bangkok 10330 • telephone: +66.22.639 333 • facsimile: +66.22.639 300 • website: www.marriott.com/bkker

PHOTOGRAPHS COURTESY OF THE MAYFAIR MARRIOTT EXECUTIVE APARTMENTS.

The Oriental Hotel

Since 1876, The Oriental, Bangkok has served as a beacon of light and warmth on the capital city's Chao Phraya river. A landmark that represents the grandeur of Thai hospitality, The Oriental has inspired some of the world's most famous writers. Noel Coward, Somerset Maugham and Joseph Conrad have all enjoyed its sumptuous suites, distinctive ambience and distinguished service fit for royalty.

In September 2005, the completion of the multi-million-dollar restoration of The Oriental represented a new era for this Thai legend. Recognised as one of the world's premier city resorts, it retains its nostalgic charm with its magnificent colonial architectural styles and glorious landscaping.

Guests can choose to stay in one of 393 superbly appointed rooms, including 35 luxury suites, looked after by an attentive staff of over 1,000. Each guest room is exquisitely decorated with rich Thai silk fabrics, beautiful heavy woods and gilded accents. Natural light flows are unbridled.

A large part of The Oriental's heritage is in its renowned culinary experiences that date back to 1958, when Le Normandie, a French restaurant with sweeping views of the river and the city, opened its doors on the top floor of the hotel's Garden Wing.

The restaurant's tradition of hiring three-star Michelin chefs continues today. Four other restaurants—The China House, Lord Jim's, Sala Rim Naan and Ciao—serve a mouth-watering array of cuisines from Chinese, international, seafood, traditional Thai and Italian. Meanwhile, the Oriental Thai Cooking School offers lessons in fine Thai cuisine. Classes are limited to just 15 students so that personalised attention and participation are key.

The Oriental Spa, voted 'Best In The World' by *Travel & Leisure* magazine, and recently 'Best Overseas Spa 2005' by *Conde Nast Traveller*, UK, is a temple of well-being. It is set in an old teakwood house with only 14 private suites to ensure luxury and exclusivity.

The gentle spa therapists have been specially trained in the ancient art of natural Thai remedies. As befits a hotel of such stature, The Oriental also has all the modern conveniences that allow business travellers

to effectively work and play. High-speed Internet access is available in all rooms and a state-of-the-art business centre provides professional support. A luxurious fleet of BMW 7 series limousines is also available

along with experienced drivers with their reputation for courtesy. With its 130th anniversary in 2006, The Oriental's unique style, superb facilities and impeccable service are well worth celebrating.

FACTS		
ROOMS	35 suites • 358 luxuriously appointed rooms	
FOOD	Le Normandie: French • The China House: Chinese • Lord Jim's: seafood • Ciao: Italian • Sala Rim Naan: Thai • The Verandah: international • Riverside Terrace: international	
DRINK	The Bamboo Bar • Authors' Lounge	
FEATURES	The Oriental Spa • 2 pools • health centre • tennis and squash courts • jogging track • sauna • steam room • cooking school • conference facilities • high-speed Internet access • day care centre	
NEARBY	Championship golf courses • Grand Palace	
CONTACT	48 Oriental Avenue, Bangkok 10500 • telephone: +66.2.659 9000 • facsimile: +66.2.659 0000 • email: orbkk-reservations@mohg.com • website: www.mandarinoriental.com	

PHOTOGRAPHS COURTESY OF THE ORIENTAL HOTEL.

Siri Sathorn

THIS PAGE (FROM TOP): Each serviced apartment is spacious and welcoming; artwork, flowers and ornaments create a warm, homely ambience.

OPPOSITE: Sip a cocktail in the chic Liquid Bar and Café.

Serviced apartments have come a long way from the cold, sparsely furnished spaces that provided extended-stay shelter to business travellers. With boutique hotels burgeoning in cities everywhere, the service apartment has had to reinvent itself. So who better to do this than a hospitality company that has won high acclaim for its personalised service, exquisite design and top-of-the-line facilities?

As sister property to The Sukhothai hotel, Siri Sathorn, a Beaufort serviced residence, is truly a chic home away from home. Stylishly appointed and designed to make the very best use of space, Siri Sathorn is fast becoming the serviced residence of choice for discerning executives. At first glance, it would be easy to mistake Siri Sathorn for a stylish boutique hotel.

Sleek designer furnishings, thoughtfully placed lighting, high-speed Internet access and quality entertainment systems complement a bevy of staff who are at your service 24 hours a day.

Marble and mirrors make up the main theme of the apartments' decor.

Marble and mirrors make up the main theme of the apartments' décor. Warm and homely, they each come with individual air-conditioning, hair dryers, steam irons, direct telephone lines, voice mail and facsimile lines.

Located on Soi Saladaeng 1, a quiet and safe street close to the junction of Silom, Sathorn and Rama IV Road, Siri Sathorn is conveniently within walking distance of the Saladaeng Skytrain station and Silom MRT station, Lumpini Park and shopping malls. Yet with its double-glazed windows in all apartments, guests are shielded from the noise of the city outside. Can't sleep? The famed Patpong area is a mere stone's throw away. Stroll over for a midnight snack and hop on a tuk tuk home when the bustle of nightlife gets the better of you.

Residents and guests are free to use the property's state-of-the-art fitness club, as well as its meeting rooms and business centre free of charge. Morning brings with it a complimentary English-language newspaper at each doorstep and an American buffet breakfast at Siri Sathorn's Liquid Bar and Café. Throughout the day, the café serves outstanding Thai and Western cuisine, and

by night, it becomes a hip bar to chill out in with friends. Of course, if you feel like staying in after a hard day's work, Siri Sathorn also offers room service until 11 pm. With spoilings like these it's hard to leave.

FACTS		
ROOMS	111 suites	
FOOD	Liquid Bar and Café: Western and Thai • outdoor pool garden: Thai	
DRINK	Liquid Bar and Café	
FEATURES	fitness centre • spa • business centre • free shuttle bus to Silom Rd, shops and trains • swimming pool • high-speed Internet access • jacuzzi • meeting rooms • private dining room with karaoke	
NEARBY	Patpong • Lumpini Park • Saladaeng Skytrain station • Silom MRT station • Suanlum Night Bazaar	
CONTACT	27 Soi Saladaeng 1, Silom Road, Silom, Bangrak, Bangkok 10500 • telephone: +66.2.266 2345 • facsimile: +66.2.267 5555 • email: reservation@sirisathorn.com • website: www.sirisathorn.com	

PHOTOGRAPHS COURTESY OF SIRI SATHORN.

Swissôtel Nai Lert Park Bangkok

THIS PAGE: *Contemporary elegance in the spacious rooms.*

OPPOSITE: *Innovative dining concepts at Syn Bar and Iso. Colour and light complement the respective themes, along with good food and drink.*

Having recently undergone a 10-month renovation programme, Swissôtel Nai Lert Park Bangkok exudes contemporary elegance. Set in a sprawling garden estate in the heart of Bangkok's central business district, this five-star hotel is plush with graceful interiors that echo beautifully the richness of its luxurious surroundings.

Ivory-white doors lead to its new guest rooms and suites that come with bright, airy bathrooms and spacious balconies, overlooking all 3.5 hectares (8.5 acres) of its picturesque gardens. Polished woods in warm reds and dark browns lift the décor's sophisticated base of grey, beige and ecru, evoking an air of swish comfort. The centerpiece of each room is a pair of 'Mamma and Pappa' armchairs specially designed by acclaimed New York architect Calvin Tsao. These chic ergonomic works of art are representative of the hotel's design philosophy that every single decorative item forms an aesthetic yet functional contrast to the clean, clear lines of the rooms' furnishings. Indeed, art and comfort are entwined throughout Nai Lert.

The hotel's three wings are comprised of four floors each, all decked out in minimalist lines and focusing on expertly blended colour. Its lobby is dotted with plush mustard and pimento armchairs, softened by shades of biscuit and wood furnishings. It is here that new guests are welcomed in, receiving their first taste of the famed Swissôtel service and often admiring the impressive art installations which frame their entrance. Meanwhile, Nai Lert Park's Garden Wing on the ground floor has been left bare, save for a stunning elevated seating area where amazing bead chairs are suspended from the ceilings and floors, creating a strangely futuristic Zen-like atmosphere.

No five-star hotel is complete without outstanding dining concepts to satiate the appetites of its hungriest and most discerning guests. Nai Lert Park caters perfectly with a host of fine restaurants that offer some of the best cuisine in the whole of Bangkok. Of note is Iso, located beneath the hotel's lobby. As it opens up to the opulent garden area, Iso's large glass frontage allows a flood of natural light to stream through, rendering the shades of emerald and brown from the greenery outside brighter and yet more vibrant. Fusion is the key to ingredients here as Iso, which means 'equal' in Greek, serves mouthwatering Western and Pan-Asian dishes.

The main attraction for Bangkok city-types is Nai Lert Park's über-cool Syn Bar, where the chic and stylish come to unwind and enjoy its signature cocktails. Encased cleverly in glass, Syn fuses furniture design from the last three decades with a space-age DJ booth, iconic bubble chairs and clever lighting that melts ethereally from one colour to the next. Suffice to say, hip has never looked this good in Bangkok.

Colour and light complement the respective themes, along with good food and drink that delights the tastebuds and wraps the evening in a satisfied glow. Resident Syn DJs spin an irresistible blend of chill-out and funk tunes, which conspire with the sparkling fibre-optic carpets to evoke a feeling of floating under a thousand stars. Then again, it could just be the gently blurring effects of one of Bennie's unique creations like the Bai Toey Martini, Mangosteen Martini and Tamarind Passion. No wonder the hip parade descend here to sink into Syn's bubble chairs and sofas all evening long. From 5 pm until 9 pm during the week, Syn celebrates the end of the workday with 50 per cent off standard drinks and selected cocktails. Meanwhile, Thursday nights at Syn play host to Bangkok's coolest Hospitality evening. 'Industry Night' as it is called, boasts the inimitable DJ Pound at the funky decks and 50 per cent off standard drinks and cocktails for happy hours lasting the entire night.

THIS PAGE (FROM TOP): Bathrooms are elegant in clean white and simple lines; relax by the pool while the city bustles outside.

OPPOSITE: Wide, spacious atriums, and lush serene gardens are a respite from the city crowds outside the walls.

Stay active and healthy with the Amrita Fitness facilities situated within the Nai Lert itself. Ample pathways wind around the extensive gardens so energetic guests can jog in the pleasures of the cool green grounds. Indulge in a spa treatment or two before luxuriating in the sauna or steam room. The options are endless, with squash and tennis courts, aerobics rooms and top-of-the-line fitness equipment.

Nearby, Bangkok's exciting shopping and entertainment areas beckon those with a thirst for exploration. Sign up for a sightseeing excursion with the hotel or contact the concierge to put together your own personalised tour of the city. Business travellers will appreciate Nai Lert Park Bangkok's Executive Club services, which feature 24-hour butler service and in-room espresso machines, as well as complimentary breakfast, tea and cocktails at the Executive Club Lounge. With services and amenities like these, it's hard to leave.

PHOTOGRAPHS COURTESY OF SWISSÔTEL NAI LERT PARK BANGKOK.

FACTS		
ROOMS	338 rooms and suites	
FOOD	Ma Maison: French • Genji: Japanese • Noble House: Cantonese • Gourmandises: pastries and snacks • iso: western and Asian, Pool Bar: snacks	
DRINK	Syn Bar • Pool Bar	
FEATURES	spa • aerobics room • squash court • tennis court • sauna rooms • executive club floor • Internet access • conference facilities	
NEARBY	Central World Plaza • business and diplomatic district • Gaysorn Plaza	
CONTACT	2 Wireless Road, Bangkok 10330 • telephone: +66.2.253 0123 • facsimile: +66.2.254 8740 • email: reservations@nailertpark.swissotel.com • website: www.nailertpark.swissotel.com	

The Sukhothai Bangkok

THIS PAGE (CLOCKWISE FROM TOP LEFT): *Dine in style at one of the hotel's acclaimed restaurants; an extensive pillow menu guarantees a good night's rest; a tastefully designed room; guestrooms overlook courtyards and peaceful water gardens.*
OPPOSITE: *A spectacular pool takes centrestage.*

The 13th-century capital city of Sukhothai was renowned for its architectural grace and peaceful populace. Fittingly, its namesake hotel takes its design cues from the ancient city to combine luxury and impeccable service with rich history and culture. Situated off the bustling Sathorn Road in Bangkok's business district, this five-star hotel spreads over 2.5 hectares (6.2 acres) and features 210 rooms and suites in an enclave of low-rise buildings. Stunning décor and architecture aside, its low-rise buildings are precisely what sets The Sukhothai apart in a city studded with high-rise hotels.

A sense of space and light permeates the property, serving as a peaceful counterpoint to the busy city outside. Numerous tranquil water features distinguish the hotel grounds, reflecting like mirrors the white walls of the main building and the pavilion outhouses.

Balanced symmetry is the order of The Sukhothai's beautiful design. Long processional halls are lined simply with Sukhothai-style art and sculptures, and flower gardens fill its open-air arcades.

If you've ever wondered where the minimalist-Asian trend that has pervaded boutique hotels all over the region took root,

you'll only have to look here. In The Sukhothai's rooms, sensual simplicity spills into its décor which prominently features teak and shades of pale jade. Mirrors increase the feeling of space while textural fabrics lend a sumptuous elegance.

The height of Sukhothai luxury can be experienced in the spectacular Sukhothai Suite, which features a baby grand piano, a fully-equipped kitchen and a 25 sq m (269 sq ft) bathroom with a silk-covered chaise in the centre of the teakwood floor. It is therefore no surprise to learn that the likes of Ricky Martin and Australia's Prime Minister John Howard have spent more than a night here.

The Sukhothai is known as much for its five-star hospitality as it is for its excellent dining options. The Celadon is undoubtedly its most highly acclaimed restaurant. Housed in a picturesque sala in the centre of a lake of lotuses, this Thai restaurant is consistently rated one of the best in the city and draws international visitors and savvy locals alike. An extensive wine list, featuring top wines from around the globe, complements its award-winning menu.

As befits a hotel of such distinguished stature, The Sukhothai's service is unfailingly warm. With IT butlers to an extensive pillow menu on offer, it's easy to feel at home. Still, if you fancy a little more relaxation, or you are suffering the effects of jet-lag, a visit the hotel's multi-million-dollar spa is a must. Indulge in one of the signature massages with aromatic oils and feel your worries melt away. And when you're ready, the excitement and energy of the buzzing city of Bangkok awaits at your doorstep.

PHOTOGRAPHS COURTESY OF THE SUKHOTHAI BANGKOK.

FACTS	
ROOMS	82 suites • 128 rooms
FOOD	The Colonnade: International • The Celadon: Fine Thai • La Scala: Italian
DRINK	Pool Terrace Café and Bar • Lobby Salons • The Zuk Bar
FEATURES	pool • spa • health club • jacuzzi • sauna • steam bath • whirlpool and massage facilities • aerobics classes • squash court • tennis court • business centre • meeting and conference facilities • boutiques
NEARBY	Lumpini Park • Snake Farm • Skytrain and subway stations • embassies • shops
CONTACT	13/3 South Sathorn Road, Bangkok 10120 • telephone: +66.23.448 888 • facsimile: +66.23.448 899 • email: info@sukhothai.com • website: www.sukhothai.com

i.sawan Residential Spa + Club

Quietude, peace and a slower pace can sometimes seem a world away, but today, in the heart of Bangkok, one oasis of calm offers a rejuvenating retreat.

i.sawan Residential Spa & Club is tucked away in the garden of the famed Grand Hyatt Erawan Bangkok. This "fifth level of heaven"—so named because of its terrace location on the fifth floor of the hotel—is spread over 7,000 sq m (75,347 sq ft) and possesses all the luxuries and comforts needed to relieve guests of stress and strain. A virtual garden in the sky, i.sawan was created as a special indulgence for those seeking a higher sense of well-being. This ultimate spa hideaway fuses the power of science and nature to develop timeless and healing treatments to restore your inner calm and balance.

i.sawan's experienced staff have dedicated themselves to providing only the best therapeutic experiences, from

...a special indulgence for those seeking a higher sense of well being.

massages and reflexology to skincare treatments, and health and beauty services.

Stay in one of six Residential Spa Cottages lined up along a gently winding path. Each has been thoughtfully designed as a home away from home, where the sounds of the city give way to the melodies of nature—birds, breeze and gentle water.

Representing a brand new concept of hospitality in Bangkok, these cottages, each consisting of a bedroom, living room, bathroom, outdoor patio and private treatment room, allow guests to indulge in the harmony of i.sawan while enjoying exquisite spa treatments in the privacy of their own accommodation. Nine other Bungalows, all appointed in contemporary style with subtle Thai accents, offer equally sumptuous comforts amidst a landscape inspired by the beauty of Provence.

Enjoy quiet walks along pathways edged with hedgerows, pea gravel and frangipani trees, or spend the afternoon relaxing by the pool. If the yen for activity strikes, head to The Greenhouse, where a glass-fronted state-of-the-art gym raises your heart rate, while sunlight streams through like beams of good energy. A tennis court and two squash courts will satisfy the competitive-spirited, but if calm is more your cup of tea, there are also yoga and holistic fitness classes. Then retire to the Juice Bar for a sweet, healthy reward. Indeed, urban renewal is rarely this good.

PHOTOGRAPHS COURTESY OF I.SAWAN RESIDENTIAL SPA + CLUB.

FACTS		
ROOMS	6 residential spa cottages • 3 treatment bungalows with terrace • 6 treatment bungalows	
FOOD	The Breezeway: open-air casual cuisine	
DRINK	Juice Bar	
FEATURES	spa • swimming pool • squash • tennis • gym • nail bar • hair salon • fitness studio	
NEARBY	Erawan Shrine • Central World Plaza • Erawan Bangkok Boutique Mall • Lumpini Park	
CONTACT	5th floor, Grand Hyatt Erawan Bangkok, 494 Rajdamri Road, Bangkok 10330 • telephone: +66.2.254 6310 • facsimile: +66.2.254 6283 • email: isawan.ghbangkok@hyattintl.com • website: www.bangkok.grand.hyatt.com	

Sareerarom Tropical Spa

In the heart of bustling Bangkok lies a sanctum of calm. Sareerarom Tropical Spa is an oasis of good health, where holistic well-being is nurtured through personalised health consultations, beauty therapy and body treatments.

Enter the spa and your senses relax. Vastly different from the throbbing city outside, you will find lush gardens verdant with tropical plants and flowers, surrounded by an open-air terrace. It feels like an exotic tropical garden resort, a sanctuary from the stresses of everyday life. Inside, bamboo shutters create ethereal curtains that shield you from the world. The walls are awash in soft, creamy hues, while vibrant shades of vermilion Thai silk bestow a richness to dark wood furnishings. The sound of birdsong and the fragrance of aromatic oils provide a calming backdrop for those in search of private indulgence.

True to its name—Sareera means 'physical', while Arom refers to the mind and emotions—Sareerarom offers a spectrum of treatments designed especially for its spa, based on traditional Thai massage as a foundation for healing and relaxing the body. Highly experienced Thai therapists are on hand to identify your sore spots and knotted muscles. After the delightful massage, your tensions are eased, allowing vital positive energy to resume its free flow

THIS PAGE (FROM TOP): Organic ingredients promote health from within; the Saree Tea Room pays charming attention to detail; a Sareerarom therapist works her soothing magic.
OPPOSITE: Pick up a magazine, lie back and soak up the exotic gardens around you.

throughout your body. Some of the spa's most popular treatments are the Rice Bran Body Scrub, Asian Blend Massage and Sareerarom Aromatherapy Massage.

To further relax, settle into the Saree Tea Room, an inviting retreat that feels much like the living room of a very stylish friend. With deep purple walls, the Tea Room is softened by the glow of candles. Its design is comfortingly eclectic—a mix of Japanese, Indian, Chinese and European motifs and textures. Open from 10 am until 10 pm, the Tea Room serves a selection of the best teas from around the world, as well as a range of scrumptious snacks like home-baked cakes, soft buttery scones, open-faced sandwiches and Chinese moon cakes. Surrender to chill-out tunes and browse the selection of international books and magazines, or maybe pick up a treat from the spa's shop. After hours of relaxation in this temple of serenity, step back out into the city and experience the everyday anew.

PHOTOGRAPHS COURTESY OF SAREERAROM TROPICAL SPA.

FACTS

ROOMS	spa treatment rooms
FOOD	Saree Tea Room: tea and organic snacks
DRINK	Saree Tea Room
FEATURES	spa • yoga classes • The Sareerarom Spa Shop
NEARBY	prime residential area • Emporium mall
CONTACT	117 Thonglor Soi 10, Sukhumvit 55, Wattana, Bangkok 10110 • telephone: +66.2.391 9919 • facsimile: +66.2.391 9969 • email : info@sareerarom.com • website: www.sareerarom.com

Bed Supperclub

Eating in bed has never been this chic. At Bed Supperclub, arguably Bangkok's coolest designer watering hole, dinner in bed means nudging against the city's young, hip and happening.

Set in a giant cylinder of a building, Bed Supperclub is almost a parody of what was expected of the millennium by those living in the 1970s. Futuristic all-white interiors glow under blue neon lights. Futon-like chairs line the floors while daybeds are suspended from the walls.

Diners are assigned their slot on one of two big beds lining the walls. Three-course meals are ordered from a limited menu on weeknights and served on the crisply made beds, complete with fluffy white pillows and matching acrylic trays.

Led by Chef Dan Ivarie, Bed Supperclub's menu offers a unique blend of Mediterranean dishes with Asian overtones and elements of upscale American home-style cooking. Think Chilled Guava Melon Soup with Crab in Citrus Mayonnaise and Curried Apple Sorbet, or Crispy Coriander Duck Wontons with Emulsified Mushroom Jus and Soy Mustard Sauce. Small wonder that chefs around the region seek to replicate this unique cooking style, which demonstrates a true knowledge of the Asian palate.

On weekends, dinner begins at 8.30 pm sharp. Without doubt, these are

'Expect the unexpected' is the edict...

DJs provide a backdrop of music from house to chill-out grooves. Sweet endings are de rigueur here, and we're not talking of run-of-the-mill chocolate confections. Knock back cocktails specially created by Chef Ivarie, like Blueberry and Basil Mojito with Lychee Pepper Sorbet or Pandan and Mango Martinis with Shaved Coconut Vermouth Ice.

THIS PAGE (FROM TOP): The sleek modern bar, where over 20 signature cocktails are created; the surreal futuristic cylinder of the Bed Supperclub's exterior.
OPPOSITE: Amidst stark minimalist white and neon lighting, you are served dinner in your crisply-made bed.

no ordinary meals—the weekend special surprise four-course menu is served in only one sitting, with unique entertainment to engage guests. 'Expect the unexpected' is the edict on these occasions. Singers, dancers, interactive performers and artists, or a host of talents from anywhere in the world could grace each course of your dinner in bed, with the dessert performance being a special highlight.

Watch the food being prepared in the open kitchen, while Thai and international

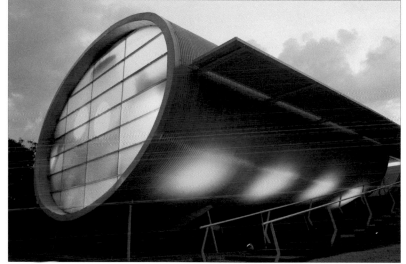

FACTS

FOOD	Mediterranean, American regional and Asian
DRINK	Bed Bar • restaurant
FEATURES	beds with oversized pillows for dining from • cylindrical exterior • open kitchen
NEARBY	prime residential area •Emporium mall
CONTACT	26 Sukhumvit Soi 11, Sukhumvit Road, Klongoey-Nua, Wattana, Bangkok, 10110 • telephone: +66.2.651 3537 • facsimile: +66.2.651 3538 • email: info@bedsupperclub.com • website: www.bedsupperclub.com

PHOTOGRAPHS COURTESY OF BED SUPPERCLUB.

Face

THIS PAGE (FROM TOP): *Face is a welcoming oasis set in traditional Thai houses; intricate wooden panels in the Face spa; sweeping ceilings in Lan Na Thai restaurant.*

OPPOSITE: *A stunning sculpture of the mystical Garuda and an ornate carving add exotic flair to the Hazara restaurant.*

In the days of the Silk Route, caravans were the primary source of travel for merchants plying the towns and deserts between Europe and China. Along the way, caravansaries served as their shelters and welcoming rest stops, open to travel-weary traders from all corners of the globe. Inspired by the romance and harmony of this bygone era, Face Bar in Bangkok was built.

Set in a pair of traditional frame houses tucked away in a serene garden off Bangkok's bustling Sukhumvit Road, Face is really a complex that comprises two restaurants, a bar, a spa, as well as a European pastry shop. Diversity is indeed the order of this complex. Face is a like a contemporary caravansary, lovingly appointed with a sensual, lively ambience that encourages its worldly patrons to meet, eat, drink and talk.

Upon arrival, guests are invited to enjoy a drink at Face Bar, where, if it suits your fancy, you may sip your tipple Thai-style, sitting cross-legged on the floor. Or perhaps you would like to sink into a supple leather armchair, or drape yourself on one of the ornate Chinese opium beds, slipping into a reverie of the days of wandering caravans.

For the famished soul, the complex presents two magnificent restaurants. Hazara, set by a tranquil koi pond serves beautiful northern Indian cuisine, and Lan Na Thai offers exceptional Thai cuisine.

Hazara, named after a tribe and region in Afghanistan, offers a blend of healthy country cooking and rich courtly cuisine. Its sensual atmosphere is enlivened by Balinese sculptures, presided over by a 3 m (10 ft) sculpture of Garuda, the beloved Hindu bird-god. At Lan Na Thai, the food mirrors the surrounding city, with dishes like duck with kaffir lime leaves, coconut shrimp and the ever-popular Paad Thai, superbly made.

For those with a sweet tooth, a visit to the complex's patisserie and café, Visage, is essential. Watch in awe as pastry chef Eric Perez, whose stellar resume includes stints with the French embassy and the Ritz in Washington DC, creates fresh chocolates

and decadent pastries daily. How could you possibly resist these luscious treats?

Meanwhile, the new Face Spa offers invigorating massages to pamper the weary traveller's mind, body and spirit. Richly set with antiques and objets d'art fit for a

museum, the spa is the perfect spot to bliss out in the heart of Thailand's bustling capital before getting ready for a night on the town. Of course, with two fabulous restaurants and an elegant bar, a night on the town means you really don't need to go very far.

FACTS

FOOD	Hazara: north Indian • Lan Na Thai: Thai • Visage: desserts and pastries
DRINK	Face Bar • Visage: café
FEATURES	spa • classic teak house in mixed Lan Na and Ayutthaya styles
NEARBY	Emporium Mega Mall • Thong Lo Station
CONTACT	29 Soi 38 Sukhumwit Rd, Phrakhanong, Klongtoey, Bangkok 10110 • telephone: +66.27.186.048 • facsimile: +66.27.186.047 • email: ravi@facebars.com • website: www.facebars.com

Vertigo Grill + Moon Bar

Like all Banyan Tree properties, the Banyan Tree Bangkok sits like an oasis of calm amidst the hustle and bustle of the Thai capital. Enter its doors and the soft, comforting scent of exotic lemongrass permeates your being, evoking a rich and immediate sense of serenity and relaxation.

Just 30 minutes away from Bangkok International Airport, the Banyan Tree Bangkok is the only all-suite hotel in the heart of the City of Angels, and boasts the tallest garden spa. The building it occupies soars up to 61 floors, and right at the apex of this arresting structure is the Vertigo Grill and Moon Bar. Shortly after it opened, Vertigo was awarded the Best New Restaurant Award 2002 by *Bangkok Dining and Entertainment* magazine.

At sunset, this sprawling space under the stars comes alive, as guests arrive to watch the brilliant shades of crimson transform into the darkness of night.

...the restaurant affords a stunning 360-degree view of the city...

Set on a former helipad, the restaurant affords an outstanding 360-degree view of the city, with glittering landmarks—behold the Grand Palace twinkling in gold, the Royal Chapel, the Chao Phraya river, Wat Pho temple, National Museum and the serene Emerald Buddha.

Thanks to this stunning landscape, an excellent team of service staff and a mouth-watering menu of international cuisine, the Vertigo Grill and Moon Bar has become a favourite haunt for visitors from every corner of the world. Able to seat up to 100 guests, Vertigo is divided into three sections—a cosy and romantic dining courtyard, a hip private party lounge, and the sultry Moon Bar for cocktail chill-out sessions under the stars. So popular is this venue that some of the city's most glamorous parties and events, from fashion launches to birthday celebrations, have been held here.

The cuisine of the Vertigo Grill and Moon Bar matches its spectacular views, with dishes like Red Mullet En Papillote with Thyme, Grilled Oysters with Parmesan Cheese and Mediterranean tapas, guaranteed to tantalise the tastebuds and lift the spirits. Most of its creations encompass barbecue items—straight from the grill onto your plate. All these are best enjoyed with a glass of fine champagne, wine or cocktails, as you watch the panoramic setting sun disappear below the lights of Thailand's capital city.

THIS PAGE (FROM TOP): Sip on champagne or smoke a Havana as you view glittering landmarks through a telescope.
OPPOSITE (FROM TOP): The menu is as exciting as the stunning views at sunset.

FACTS
FOOD Continental • fresh grilled seafood and barbecue items
DRINK private lounge • Moon Bar
FEATURES stunning views of Bangkok
NEARBY Banyan Tree Spa Bangkok
CONTACT Banyan Tree Bangkok, 21/100 Sathorn Road, Bangkok 10120 • telephone: +66.2.679 1200 • facsimile: +66.2.679 1199 • email: bangkok@banyantree.com • website: www.banyantree.com

PHOTOGRAPHS COURTESY OF BANYAN TREE BANGKOK.

Jim Thompson Retail Stores + Restaurants

The name Jim Thompson has been associated with the finest Thai silk products since 1947, when James H W Thompson began his mission to save the dying craft of silk hand-weaving. Captivated by the alluring beauty and lustre of the fabrics, the American entrepreneur set off to New York from Thailand, hoping to market the handwoven silks to sophisticated buyers. His idea worked; people fell in love with the fabrics and thus, Jim Thompson's famous Thai Silk Company was born.

Since then, Jim Thompson's name has evolved into an internationally acclaimed brand. Today, the Thai Silk Company has 18 retail outlets in Bangkok and 15 more around Thailand. Its global network includes shops in Singapore, Malaysia, Brunei, Melbourne, Tokyo and Dubai, plus representatives in 30 other countries.

Renowned for its innovative design using only the best Thai silks, the Jim Thompson team keeps abreast of world design and fashion trends by introducing fresh new colours every season. Working with Thai designer Ou Baholyodhin, 'Living With Jim Thompson' offers a refreshing approach to interior design and strikes a perfect balance between functionality and aesthetic appeal.

Fabric details are kept simple so the focus can remain on the fine craftsmanship. Washable cottons, durable linens, raw and unwoven silk make up a collection featuring contemporary interpretations of Jim Thompson's original bestselling designs. Within this collection are elegant garments and understated fashion accessories.

Visitors can also experience the legacy of Jim Thompson's famous hospitality if they

THIS PAGE: Stylish accessories designed to complement chic lifestyles.
OPPOSITE: The strikingly modern Thompson Bar and Restaurant at Jim Thompson's famous house on the Klong.

choose to dine at Thompson Bar and Restaurant, located in the Thai building just next to the Jim Thompson House Museum; Café 9 in the Surawong Road retail outlet or at Saladaeng Café, a standalone restaurant on Saladaeng Road.

Graced with a sumptuous array of Thai favourites inspired by his renowned dinner parties and served up with Thai-style hospitality, the restaurants keep the popular host's memory alive. Feasting on Thai delights in an elegant setting is surely the next best thing to travelling back in time and dining at Jim Thompson's famous table in his house on the Klong.

As in ancient times, modern-day travellers to the Thai kingdom often return home laden with fine silk pieces. Gifts of silk are a traditionally Thai way of honouring loved ones. So, after enjoying lunch or dinner, you can browse the collections further for a gorgeous gift for that special someone.

FACTS

FOOD	Thompson Bar and Restaurant: Thai • Saladaeng Café: Thai • Café 9: Thai
DRINK	Thompson Bar • Cafe 9
PRODUCTS	Thai silk • handmade fashion collections and accessories • interior and lifestyle products
CONTACT	96 Soi Peungmee 29, Bangchak, Prakanong, Bangkok 10260 • Thompson Bar and Restaurant: Jim Thompson House Museum, 6 Soi Kasemsan 2, Rama 1 Road, Bangkok 10330 • Saladaeng Café: 120/1 Saladaeng Soi 1, Silom Road, Bangkok 10500 • Café 9: 9 Surawong Road, Bangkok 10500 • telephone: +66 2762 2600 • facsimile: +66 2762 2609 • email: office@jimthompson.com • website: www.jimthompson.com

The Jim Thompson House

Jim Thompson is probably best remembered as the man who introduced Thai silk to the world. However, he also etched his name into Thai cultural history when he constructed a home for himself honouring the best of traditional Thai architecture. He did this on a grand scale by combining six antique teak houses— most of which were at least 200 years old —that were carefully dismantled and brought to the present site from as far away as the old capital of Ayutthaya.

A stickler for authenticity, Thompson ensured that the appropriate Thai house-building rituals were performed at every stage. First, nine Buddhist priests presided over the raising of the initial wooden pillar. Secondly, a suitable location for the all-important Thai spirit house—which shelters the spirits that watch over the land—needed

...guests to this museum can witness traditional Thai design rarely seen today.

to be found. With the spirits appeased and their favour sought, work on the house began on September 13, 1958.

Guests to this museum can appreciate a traditional Thai design rarely seen today. Steep roofs and broad overhangs protect the house's interior from the elements. Raised thresholds strengthen the walls and symbolically protect the house by keeping evil spirits from entering. Interior lighting is provided by opulent chandeliers (now electrified) which belong to a past era, having come from the 18th- and 19th-century palaces of Bangkok.

Like most Thai houses of its time, the Jim Thompson house was built facing the canal. Guests arrive through its lofty entrance hall,

at the rear of the house. The interior is richly decorated with a collection of traditional Thai paintings on wood, cloth and paper. Most of these paintings depict the life of Buddha and were created by anonymous

priest-painters or commissioned laymen who painted them as an act of religious devotion. Though originally intended as tools in religious instruction rather than works of art, these paintings are exquisite. They invariably capture the attention and imagination of visitors when they first enter the home.

The dining room, where Thompson hosted many a stylish soirée, was once part of a structure found in the village of Pak Hai on the Chao Phraya river. Its two magnificent carved tables, originally used for gaming in the late 19th century, bear the insignia of King Chulalongkorn (who reigned in 1868-1910). Of course, the chairs are covered in exquisite Thai silk, as befits the home of the man who introduced its beauty to the world. Also displayed is blue-and-white Chinese export porcelain from Ayutthaya, Indonesia and the Philippines.

THIS PAGE: *The Art Centre has rotating exhibitions focusing on textiles and contemporary arts.*

OPPOSITE: *Vibrant colours of Thai textiles, where traditional forms undergo a modern twist.*

Perhaps the most impressive part of the Jim Thompson house is the cavernous drawing room. This building dates back to about 1800. Thompson is said to have admired it on his daily visits to the weaving village of Bang Krua across the Klong Maha Nag canal. When he finally acquired the building, Thompson had it painstakingly taken apart and then lovingly reassembled at its new site. The walls were then reversed so that the carved panels under the window faced inwards. Some of the side windows were also converted to niches in which objects—like intricate wooden figures from Amarapura presented to Thompson by the Burmese government in the 1950s—could be displayed. One side of the room offers views of the lush, jungle-like garden with a terrace paved with 17th-century bricks from Ayutthaya. Beyond this terrace is a traditional Thai sala that no doubt once provided Thompson with an al fresco sanctuary to reflect and relax.

In the study are more works of art, including what some consider the most beautiful in the collection: a standing limestone Buddha from the early Dvravati School, dating back to the 8th century. This intimate room would have been an inspiring place for Thompson to read, or to write letters to his extensive network of friends.

In the beautiful bedroom, a carved teak bed with coverings of the finest Thai silk was where Thompson slept. And even Thompson's pet mice had their own stylish antique house, fashioned as an intricate and colourful wooden maze by Chinese artisans in early 19th-century Bangkok. One visitor was so inspired after seeing it that he wrote a children's book: *The Mouse House*.

In 1967, on a holiday with friends to the Cameron Highlands, Malaysia, Thompson mysteriously disappeared when he went for a walk in the surrounding jungle. Not a single clue has been found in the ensuing years as to what might have happened to this exceptional man who dedicated much of his life to Thai culture.

In 2003, another extension of the house opened its doors to the public. The Art Centre at the Jim Thompson House is located in the same compound and features rotating exhibitions on textiles and contemporary art. Designed by the Paris-based architect Christian Duc, this state-of-the-art gallery boasts over 200 sq m (2,153 sq ft) of museum and exhibition space. Indeed, both the House and the Art Centre serve as a lasting reminder of Thompson's visionary creativity and his deep love for his adopted country. It seems that his spirit lives on.

FACTS

FEATURES museum comprising six original traditional Thai teak houses • drawing room dating back to 1800 • the Mouse House • antiques • The Art Centre

FOOD Thompson Bar and Restaurant: Thai

DRINK Thompson Bar

NEARBY Chao Phraya river • historical temples and palaces • Lumpini Park • Erawan Shrine

CONTACT 6 Kasemsan Soi 2, Rama 1 Road, Bangkok 10330 • telephone: +66 22.167 368 • facsimile: +66 26 12 3744 • email: supicha@jimthompsonhouse.com • website: www.jimthompsonhouse.com

PHOTOGRAPHS BY HANS FONK, COURTESY OF THE JIM THOMPSON THAI SILK COMPANY.

Lamont Antiques + Contemporary Shops

Lamont Antiques and Contemporary comprises four luxurious galleries in some of Thailand's most elegant shopping venues. Founded by Englishman Alex Lamont, it specialises in two distinct yet complementary areas of Asian style. The first encompasses top quality Asian antiques, while the second embraces contemporary furniture and decorative accessories handcrafted in accordance with Asia's very finest traditions and materials.

Lamont's first shops opened in Bangkok's prestigious Gaysorn Plaza. In 2002 Lamont Contemporary made its debut to rave reviews for both its Zen-like interiors and finely finished products. Unique banana leaf frames, an exotic Ethopian rhino-hide disc, and boxes in pastel-coloured, rare shagreen (stingray leather) were just a few items from the unique collection, melding contemporary forms with traditional artisans' techniques. Lamont's innovative designs always impress, whether in fashion capitals like New York and Milan, or in the Asian hub of Bangkok.

A collection of unique pieces, melding the contemporary with traditional artisans' techniques.

Lamont Antiques Gallery followed shortly after. An experienced antiques dealer, Alex Lamont travelled across Asia in search of antiques, and also brought craftsmen from France and England to establish his own workshops in Bangkok for Lamont's contemporary product line. The antiques are selected for their rare qualities.

"To me, the form and texture is paramount," Alex explains. "I look for something that has a sense of beauty and authenticity. Not something obvious. A good eye can tell a fake even without experience in that field, but seeing the rare forms is more difficult." His approach demonstrates just how and why his Lamont Antiques Gallery stands apart from others in the city.

Supported by a team of attentive and knowledgeable staff, Lamont Antiques Gallery draws international customers with its excellent range of products, high ceilings, and rich textured walls, all of which endow a wonderful gravity and context to the objects and furniture displayed.

In 2003, the Lamont Collections store opened at The Oriental Hotel in Bangkok. Lamont was initially asked to design and produce room accessories for the hotel's Garden Wing renovation. So pleased was the hotel with Lamont's creations, that they invited him to open a store in its Authors' Wing, showcasing the rarest pieces and antiques in his line.

In 2004, the Lamont Phuket shop opened in the stylish new Surin Plaza, situated in the posh neighbourhood that is home to the island's most exclusive resorts—the Amanpuri, The Chedi, and Twinpalms. This spacious new shop allowed Lamont to create a different, contemporary space with a warmer atmosphere. Here, larger furniture is on offer, as are dramatic sculptures which command attention. For Lamont, it proved to be a highly successful experiment in

blending antiques with contemporary items in one venue.

Alex Lamont's taste for quality and good design can be traced to his childhood. Born into a family of antique dealers, Lamont was raised in Kenya and India before returning to England in 1975. At that time, western tastes in art and design were widening, and works from other cultural traditions were gaining popularity. So Lamont's father started a business which imported folk art from across the globe. Alex Lamont was employed in the warehouse, and through receiving items as exotic as thorn carvings from Nigeria, papier-mâché from Mexico and baskets from Bolivia, he developed a keen eye for fine craftmanship.

Over the years, Lamont accompanied his father on buying trips, learning the intricacies of patina and quality, while

...one of the leaders in Thailand's decorative arts.

After completing his studies, Lamont started his own antique Turkish carpet and kilim business, and spent five years managing Altfield, Hong Kong's premier antique dealers. But the call of Thailand proved the strongest of his passions, and Lamont decided to combine his love for Asian antiques with his love for the country that had captured his heart.

Thus, Lamont Antiques and Contemporary was born. Today, it is one of the leaders in Thailand's decorative arts. 90 per cent of all the items sold at Lamont Contemporary were created by them and if ever a particular design is copied, Lamont will make sure the piece is removed from the collection and discontinued. Indeed, there are very few large shops anywhere else in the world that can claim so much homegrown design and originality. For Lamont, offering style, authenticity and quality is of the utmost importance. He says, "My name is on the door, so I have to get it right."

developing a wide network from Turkey to Japan. Lamont travelled extensively but Thailand captured his imagination, inspiring him to undertake a degree in Thai Studies and Anthropology at London's School of Oriental and African Studies. In the meantime, his family's business grew to encompass esoteric and decorative furniture from India and Southeast Asia. The growth of the business proved good style and quality transcended fashion and trends.

FACTS

PRODUCTS Asian antiques • contemporary furniture and accessories

FEATURES unique designs • exotic natural materials • highest quality craftsmanship

CONTACT Lamont Contemporary and Lamont Antiques,
3rd Floor, Gaysorn Plaza, 999, Ploenchit Road, Bangkok 10330 •
Lamont Collections, The Oriental Hotel, 48 Oriental Avenue, Bangkok 10500 •
Lamont Phuket, 2G The Plaza Surin, 5/50 Moo 3, Chern Talay, Phuket 83110 •
telephone (retail): +66.2.656 1392 • telephone (office): +66.2.656 1250 •
facsimile: +66.2.656 1251 • email: enquiries@lamont-design.com •
website: www.lamont-design.com

PHOTOGRAPHS COURTESY OF LAMONT DESIGN CO.

Kirimaya Golf Resort + Spa

THIS PAGE: *Fairways and fair weather—perfect for a long lunch on T-Grill's balcony, or a round or two of golf.*

OPPOSITE: *Enjoy a sumptuous safari lifestyle in a tent villa; make time for quiet reflection by the mirror-like pool.*

Drive two hours away from Bangkok to the edge of Thailand's Khao Yai National Park, and a whole new world emerges. One where wild elephants, tigers and more than 300 exotic species of birds call home; where evergreen hills and grasslands stretch as far as the eye can see; where the warm season brings a flurry of beautiful butterflies and the cold season breathes an ethereal mist into the lush surroundings.

Here at Kirimaya, the urban jungle seems a million miles away from this tropical forest, opulent with the touch of nature's hand, yet rich with everything that has come to be expected of the most luxurious resorts. Rising more than 400 m (1,312 ft) above the sea, the temperatures surrounding Kirimaya are refreshingly lower than in the city, rendering this the perfect spot to enjoy a round of golf or embark on an animal safari.

Kirimaya's exclusive Jack Nicklaus-designed 18-hole championship golf course is set within the forest's natural surrounds and boasts panoramic views of Khao Yai's magnificent mountains. The course ranges from 4,436 m (4,875 yd) for ladies to an incredible 6,475 m (7,115 yd) for tournaments. A single-track layout means golfers always feel like they are the only players on the course.

Watch the local wildlife up close with the experts, traverse the forest's ancient trails, or gaze at the inky night sky lit with stars like a million Christmas lights. Or if you prefer, head to the exquisite Maya Spa where natural beauty and body therapies await. Savour sumptuous body treatments like the Pure Honey and Herbal Wrap, which envelops guests in healing ingredients

...the perfect spot to enjoy a round of golf or embark on an animal safari.

blended from a recipe that has spanned generations. Or indulge in a *Maya Massage*, a fabulously fragrant experience, where essential oils are used in a signature treatment using Thai pressure massage and relaxing kneading.

Upon their return from the superb course, golfers can head for The 19th Green, a special spa package tailored to reward the spent golfer. The treatment begins with an Aromatic Steam treatment, followed by an Aromatic Bath and then a Sun Soothing Body Wrap to salve sun-kissed

skin. Calmed and relaxed, the treatment continues with a deep-tissue Golfer's Massage, designed to relieve soreness and joint pain after a long and rewarding game. Finally, your choice of facial is administered to return a radiant glow to your countenance before you head back to your stylish accommodation for a leisurely snooze.

As real and natural as the National Park outside, Kirimaya's rooms and suites are naturally decked out in materials that are a nod to its ecological concept. Hardwood flooring, bamboo daybeds and, quite

arguably the most comfortable mattresses in Thailand, complement all the expected amenities that have won Kirimaya a place in the *Conde Nast Traveler* 2005 Hot List. Each of its 52 rooms and four suites is tastefully and thoughtfully appointed with local touches and modern accents so the shift from city to luxury jungle life is as seamless as possible. Four fabulous tented villas are the ultimate in forest accommodation, with their own private indoor spa pools and deck areas that offer unobstructed views of the golf course and Khao Yai Mountain.

Meals are equally exquisite affairs, enjoyed in the Acala Restaurant, overlooking

THIS PAGE (FROM TOP): *Fringed by foliage, the spa suite is bathed in bright sunlight; an oversized bath, brimming with blossoms; warm shades and natural fabrics in the spa rooms.*

OPPOSITE: *Dine in the open at Acala restaurant, whilst admiring the great views.*

the lake and the golf course. Taking its form from an open-air northern Thai rice barn, it is the place to enjoy amazing meals by acclaimed Bangkok chef, Somboom Satheerang. Or wander to the resort's golf clubhouse, T-Grill, which also boasts spectacular views. With a fusion of Mexican and safari décor, the restaurant serves an à la carte grill menu for lunch and dinner.

For a long, quiet drink, head to the Mist Bar. Cosy, intimate and drenched in soft light, its oversized chairs beckon you to take the weight off your feet, kick back and relax.

A speciality of the resort is a collection of lifestyle experiences, cheekily named Kirimaya Sutra. Encouraging discovery of the region's offerings, each unforgettable Kirimaya Sutra encompasses multi-sensory experiences, from vineyards and cuisine, to provincial history and cultural delights. The famous Thai hospitality seems even better in Kirimaya's cool climes, leaving everyone to sport serene, contented smiles.

FACTS		
ROOMS	52 rooms • 4 suites • 4 villas	
FOOD	Acala Restaurant • T-Grill	
DRINK	Mist Bar	
FEATURES	Cable TV • wireless high-speed Internet access • golf course • conference facilities • spa	
NEARBY	Khao Yai National Park • Phi Mai Historical Park • Chokchai farm • horse riding • elephant trekking • GranMonte Winery • Pakchong night market	
CONTACT	1/3 Moo 6 Thanarat Road Moo-Si, Pakchong Nakhon Ratchasima 30130 • telephone: +66.44.426 000/099 • facsimile: +66.44.929 888 • email: book@kirimaya.com • website: www.kirimaya.com	

PHOTOGRAPHS COURTESY OF KIRIMAYA GOLF RESORT + SPA.

souththailand+easternseaboard

Cambodia

Chonburi

Phetchaburi

Pattaya
Underwater World

> Koh Samet

Hua Hin

> Dusit Resort, Hua Hin
> Evason Hideaway + Six Senses Spa at Hua Hin
> Evason Hua Hin Resort + Six Senses Spa
> Veranda Resort + Spa

Prachuapkhirikhan

Koh Chang

> Amari Emerald Cove Resort
> Dusit Resort, Pattaya

Myanmar

Gulf of Thailand

Andaman Sea

> Koh Tao

**Ao Thong Marine
National Park**

Koh Samui

> Anantara Resort + Spa Koh Samui
> SALA Samui Resort + Spa
> Sila Evason Hideaway + Spa at Samui

Suratthani

Phang Nga

Similan Islands
> The Sarojin

Khao Lak Beach

Krabi

> The Paradise Koh Yao Beach Resort + Spa

> Twinpalms Phuket
> Trisara
> Banyan Tree Phuket
> Evason Phuket Resort +
  Six Senses Spa

Koh Yao

Koh Gai

Koh Phi Phi

> Sheraton Krabi Beach Resort
> Pimalai Resort + Spa
> Rayavadee

Phuket

Trang

Trung

> Zeavola
> Costa Lanta, Krabi
> SriLanta

Koh
Lanta

> Amari Trang Beach Resort

Koh M

a unique blend of tradition and tranquillity

The map of Thailand is shaped like an elephant's head, and the country's southern region lies on what looks like the animal's trunk extending towards Malaysia. While lush farming societies make up Thailand's central and northern regions, the south of the country subsists on fishing rather than rice farming.

The southern peninsula was once part of the ancient Indonesian Srivijaya empire, which has had a lasting impact on Thai people and their religion. Southern Thais are predominantly Muslim. Around the area near the Malaysian border, the locals speak an old Malay dialect. Koh Samui and Phuket have large populations of ethnic Chinese people who emigrated from the southern Chinese island of Hainan. Foreign influences are also evident in the architecture and food of Thailand's southern provinces.

Pretty islands like Phuket and Koh Samui existed only as sleepy fishing villages for centuries, until the travel boom of the 1970s and 1980s turned them into the exciting and international resort playgrounds they are today.

food: the spice of life

Even for chilli-loving Thais, 'southern flavour' means burning hot. Southerners like their food to bite back. The region's heritage as a historical trading hub between India and Indonesia is evident in dishes like Gang Massaman. This is a favourite Thai curry that uses strongly flavoured Indian spices like cardamom, clove and cinnamon in thick gravy.

Gang Tai Pla, another famous southern curry consisting of green beans, bamboo shoots, pumpkin and fish in an orange-coloured gravy, is especially fiery. Another very popular Southern Thai dish is Khanom Jeen, made of fermented rice noodles and eaten with just about any curry topping. But the classic choice of them all is Khanom Jeen Nam Yaa, a spicy ground fish curry.

Another much-loved Thai dish adopted from a neighbouring culture is satay, which is actually an Indonesian dish of marinated meats barbecued on small skewers and savoured with a thick, spicy peanut sauce.

THIS PAGE (FROM TOP): Contemporary chic dining options abound in southern Thailand's hip hotels; Southern Gang Massaman's distinctive Indian flavor harkens from south Thailand's importance as a historical trading hub.

OPPOSITE: The stunning karst cliffs of Ao Phra Nang Bay on the Krabi peninsula give a magical glow at sunset.

the charm of shadow play

In contrast to the magnificent paintings and inspired sculptures belonging to the central and northern regions of Thailand, the southern artistic traditions are noticeably lacking in any grand tradition of visual arts.

There is a marked absence of sculptures, paintings and elaborate architecture in the south, partly because the coastal areas were not sites of great capital cities. They did not have a legacy of monarchs immortalising their reigns in paint and stone. Coastal towns and islands consisted mostly of poor fishing villages and farming areas.

Another factor was the predominant Muslim religion, which bans the representation of human images. Instead, southern Thailand is much better known for its traditional performing arts such as plays and puppetry.

The most beautiful of these is nang or shadow puppet theatre, which is derived from the region's Malay and Indonesian influences. First brought to the Malay Peninsula by Middle Eastern traders, this art form spread to Malaysia and Indonesia. It is now considered a southern art form in Thailand.

Nang is performed by manipulating puppets—flat figures cut out of dried leather hide and exquisitely carved in the elaborate style of Thai paintings. The puppets are attached to sticks and moved about between a sheet and a light source. What the audience sees are the shadows dancing behind the sheet.

There are two types of Thai shadow puppetry. The first is nang talung, named after the Phattalung province, which is similar to the Malay and Indonesian styles. It usually relates the stories from legends and classical literature, like the *Ramakien* epic and the Thai classical epic poem 'Phra Aphaimanee', as well as folk tales. Puppets represent individual characters in these stories. Nang talung is still performed at temple fairs in the south and in Bangkok for formal entertainment.

The second variation of Thai shadow puppet theatre is nang yai, meaning 'big hide'. This is because the puppets are made of much larger hides that are almost life-size. Nang yai is uniquely Thai, and it has been dying out because of lack of training,

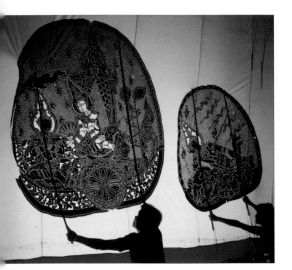

THIS PAGE: Legends and classical literature are played out using exquisite hand-carved leather shadow puppets in the dying traditional art of nang talung.

OPPOSITE (FROM TOP): You can rent a beach chair and spend the entire day soaking in the sun and surf on any of the southern coast's brilliant beaches; plentiful beach city nightlife provides a different type of heat once the sun sets.

although efforts are being made to revive it. These days, the delicate nang puppets are seen less in the theatre and more as interior design items adorning the walls of elegant homes. Puppets are also purchased for their beauty and representation of quintessential Thai craftsmanship.

holidays on the eastern seaboard

The Gulf of Thailand on the country's eastern shores has always been the local escape for city folk. It consists of a number of popular seaside resorts within a few hours' drive from Bangkok. Recently, new airports and regular flights from Bangkok to Pattaya and Hua Hin have made it even easier to jet off to the beach for a quick weekend getaway.

a bustling holiday destination

The most famous and perhaps notorious of the eastern seaboard resorts is Pattaya. Many people wistfully recall the Pattaya of their childhoods: a bay of crystal clear waters filled with fish and pristine white beaches—an image that is perhaps quite hard to reconcile with today's busy beach city.

The former fishing village has not only turned into a bustling holiday destination. Pattaya now has the dubious reputation as the stop-off point for visiting battleships— a legacy of its popularity as a rest and relaxation centre for off-duty US troops, who were stationed near the resort during the Vietnam War era.

Pattaya tends to draw mostly male visitors for its busy nightlife offerings. Don't be surprised to find that German, Arabic and Russian are the most frequently used foreign languages here; the cultures are similarly represented in many restaurant menus.

The city itself may not be the most wholesome of beach resorts, but expressway access has made it the closest and quickest beach destination from Bangkok.

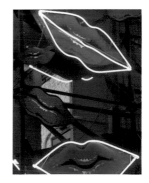

Unsurprisingly, Pattaya has, in recent years, been where Bangkok executives build their luxury second homes to indulge in golf and country weekends. Such homes can be found mostly in the Jomtien Beach area where the town is less congested, the beach much cleaner and the lifestyle more glamorous.

The best beaches are located on the many small islands in Pattaya bay, where a boat trip and a picnic lunch will transport you to a world of tranquil blue waters and plenty of privacy. Pattaya also boasts 15 golf courses and all the conveniences of modern shopping malls and movie theatres—not to mention plenty of water sports like jet-skiing, parasailing and boating. The region's most modern sea aquarium, Underwater World, is located in Pattaya.

that back-to-nature island-getaway feeling

Koh Samet is just a couple of hours' drive from Bangkok, travelling eastward past Pattaya. The small island is a popular destination for younger and more bohemian beach lovers preferring an unspoilt, back-to-nature island-getaway feeling.

Koh Samet is certainly removed from the bustling glitz of Pattaya or the glamour of Hua Hin. The Thai classical epic poem, 'Phra Aphaimanee', is set on Koh Samet. Composed by the famous poet Sunthorn Phu, the poem is the tale of an exiled prince who falls in love with a mermaid, but is kidnapped by a lovesick sea ogress. She keeps him prisoner, but he eventually defeats her by playing a magic flute. Today, you can see bronze images or paintings of this classic hero clad in princely garments, wearing a crown and playing the flute.

A national park, the island has happily remained a nature haven, both in terms of atmosphere and in attitude. It offers plenty of budget bungalow resorts and an increasing choice of more upmarket boutique ones with private ferryboats.

The laidback ambience and proximity to Bangkok make Koh Samet popular with both Thai holidaymakers and international travellers. Lazing on the island's incredibly soft white sand beaches is nothing short of heavenly.

far from the madding crowd

Koh Chang, or 'Elephant Island', is Thailand's second largest island after Phuket. It has always been an island hideaway, thanks to its distance from Bangkok and the six-hour drive on one highway. Keep going a little further on the same highway and you'll soon reach the Cambodian border. With no airport access, Koh Chang remains largely undiscovered by international travel crowds. It is, for now, the ideal spot for Thai nature lovers and a few foreigners who crave the tranquillity of an all-natural setting.

The enormous island and the surrounding 45 islands are a national park that remains unspoilt. Most of Koh Chang is covered with hills, waterfalls and jungle, with abundant wildlife and bird-watching opportunities.

THIS PAGE: Breathtakingly beautiful beaches around Phuket and Krabi make you just want to sit and stare in wonder.
OPPOSITE: Para-sailing (above) and jet-skiing (below) are among the many water sports that dominate the Pattaya beach scene.

There are now a few luxury resorts sprinkled on Koh Chang, and one can expect more to follow since the current Prime Minister, Thaksin Shinawatra, recently declared that this island should be developed into a second Phuket for the eastern seaboard. Some surrounding islands, like Koh Mak and Koh Kut, are renowned for their pure white sand and limpid coves, and have small, private bungalow resorts. Though these places require some time and patience to reach, you will be well rewarded with a heavenly idyllic seclusion all to yourself.

a royal retreat

About a three-hour drive south of Bangkok, Hua Hin has been the country's royal retreat since 1926, when King Rama VI built a summer palace there and called it Klai Kangwon, meaning 'far from worries'. Indeed, this peaceful seaside resort is steeped in royal heritage. The royal family still uses the palace as its summer retreat, and the reigning monarch has made it his permanent residence in recent years, eschewing city life for the wonderfully clean sea air.

There is also an elegant old palace in neighbouring Cha-am called Phra Ratchaniwet Marukhathayawan, a former summer abode constructed with beautiful golden teak during King Rama VI's reign. It is now a museum, with rooms connected by a series of long, airy verandas running parallel to the sea. Owing to its unusual design, the mostly open-air building enjoys the full effect of cooling breezes.

The town has also remained the summer retreat for the Thai aristocracy since the 1920s. Many old families still maintain land and beach houses in the area, so that rambling old wooden bungalows on big tracts of private property are interspersed with hotels and luxury resorts. However, many aristocrats have exchanged their wooden beach villas for luxurious contemporary condominiums.

Hua Hin was a simple country town until recent years, during which the creation of stylish new luxury resorts and golf courses brought it to the attention of the international travel and corporate crowd. With its 5-km (3-mile) stretch of perfectly flat, wide white

beaches, its salubrious air and excellent fresh seafood, Hua Hin is a favourite haunt for family holidays and golf weekends. Still, thanks to its royal patronage, the town has remained safe from the encroachment of over-commercialisation, and retains all the natural grace of its quiet rural charm.

Hua Hin's colonial legacy is embodied in the sprawling Sofitel Central Hua Hin resort, formerly known as Hua Hin Railway Beach Hotel in the 1920s, until it was taken over and renovated by new owners in the 1990s. The resort now boasts an enviable distinction for being the only colonial resort hotel in Thailand. The old-world aura of its long verandas and wide lawns makes an elegant setting for parties.

Up until a few years ago, the highlight of dining out in Hua Hin meant savouring delicious seafood at one of the many outdoor restaurants on the pier, with lights from fishing boats sparkling on the horizon as a romantic backdrop. Nowadays, a new type of chic is emerging on the waterfront, with more stylish eateries arriving on the scene—some of them in independent places such as the Chao Lay seafood restaurant on the beach; some in luxury hotels like the Anantara. This new wave of food outlets is also situated in the hip Monsoon restaurant and bar, decorated with 1920s art deco and silk Indochina-style lamps, and offering a mixed Vietnamese and Thai menu.

THIS PAGE: The Earth Spa at Evason Hideaway Hua Hin is the country's first luxury spa made of mud huts.

OPPOSITE: Hua Hin's spas offer beautifully designed interiors to compete with the beach landscape, such as these at the Evason Hideaway's Earth Spa by Six Senses (top) and the Anantara Spa (below).

Hua Hin has broken new ground with trendy boutique resorts like Veranda and Evason Hideaway. These destinations provide a fresh alternative to the bigger luxury establishments, exerting a youthful and more personal ambience popular with Bangkok yuppies in the fashion and media industries.

With all its attractions, Hua Hin has evolved into a social scene for executive Bangkok. In the past four years, it has been the headquarters for Thai elephant polo. Every September, the King's Cup Elephant Polo Tournament, a glamorous and heavily promoted week-long tournament, takes place, with international elephant polo teams flying in to compete. The action-packed matches include a celebrity tournament, with famous local people as competitors. In 2004, the Elephant Polo tournament saw 14 international teams participating on elephants, including the British Airways-sponsored team comprised of the UK's top horse polo players.

A representative from the Thai monarch is sent to grace the final ceremonies. The event culminates in a gala dinner, where CEOs and diplomats meet and mingle with wildlife conservationists and animal rights activists.

THIS PAGE: *International elephant polo has become an annual highlight of the Hua Hin social calendar.*
OPPOSITE: *Thailand's famed spas offer a fantastic range of chic design from minimalist interiors to rock-cave steam rooms.*

a veritable 'wellness' destination

Smaller than its famous sister Phuket, Koh Samui draws a younger and more bohemian crowd. Surrounded by an archipelago of 80 smaller islands, Samui is Thailand's third largest island with a tradition of coconut farming. For centuries, it was quiet, unspoilt, and covered with coconut plantations. It saw its first foreign backpackers in the 1970s.

Since then, Samui has slowly become a getaway island for backpackers. Visitors board the overnight train from Bangkok and then a ferry in order to stay in budget beach bungalows and chill out on the paradise island. The opening of an airport in 1989 meant more international travellers, and the establishment of larger luxury resorts.

Now, Samui is one of the most popular beach destinations in Southeast Asia, not least because of the famous monthly Full Moon parties held on the neighbouring island of Phang Ngan. Samui is also considered something of a wellness destination, with holistic centres and resorts offering vegetarian food, fasting help and colonic irrigation.

The more popular beaches, Chaweng and Lamai, lie on the island's eastern side and are packed with resorts and restaurants. With its busy social life, the island has advanced from its early backpacker days. Among the budget bungalows, you can now find upscale establishments such as the Sila Evason Hideaway on the northern tip, with its gorgeous views of the Gulf of Thailand. SALA Samui is a five-star villa resort for those with a thirst for luxury; while Anantara and its signature made-for-two terrazzo bathtubs provide an irresistibly romantic retreat.

swimming with sea turtles

Located 60 km (37 miles) north of Koh Samui, Koh Tao, or Turtle Island, is the place to head for if you fancy a swim with sea turtles. Here, all of the spectacular sights are underwater, not on land. The island is a mecca for scuba divers, and it caters well to the many diving and snorkelling enthusiasts who flock here. The usual route to Koh Tao is by train from Bangkok, followed by a ferry to the island, where most of the basic accommodation is of the simple bungalow type.

a hint of a mystical lagoon

Ao Thong Marine National Park circles Samui with 41 karst islets that are a kayaker's dream. This park is the setting for the Leonardo DiCaprio film *The Beach*, and it is easy to believe that a mystical lagoon could be located here. The lovely islets are a treasure trove of sea caves and hidden lagoons, jagged limestone cliffs, white sand beaches and dense jungle. An ideal way of spending a day in this park is to pack a picnic and hire a boat to take you snorkelling in the lagoons.

the west coast

Thailand's west coast lies on the Andaman Sea, and this area is the country's most scenic coastline. The most famous destinations on the Andaman coast are Phuket and the surrounding islands, which are the most spectacular in the country.

'the best island in the world'

Million-dollar holiday villas designed by Philippe Starck are adding glamour to the landscape on Thailand's undisputed star island. Phuket has long been a hot destination for the rich and famous. The tranquil seclusion of exclusive resorts is well loved, and the current trend is to own a contemporary villa on the island. After all, Paris-based fashion designer Kenzo has had one here for years. It is persistently rumoured that Naomi Campbell has one too, although no one can actually say where.

Thailand's largest island is the most popular beach escape in the region, attracting thousands each year with its award-winning resorts. Phuket itself regularly wins travel accolades and was proud to be voted 'Best Island in the World' in a readers' survey by the highly prestigious *Condé Nast Traveller Magazine*.

The most popular beaches are the enormous bays on the island's western coast. Patong is the busiest, with an active nightlife rivalling Pattaya's, and a vast selection of German, Italian and Mexican eateries. Surin Beach is more exclusive, and home to the fabulously hip hotel Twinpalms. In the same neighbourhood stands the new Surin Plaza

THIS PAGE (FROM TOP): South Thailand's myriad coral reefs are a snorkeller's paradise; brilliant white beaches are unrivalled anywhere in Southeast Asia.

OPPOSITE (FROM TOP): Hundreds of southern islands are perfect for exploring, just take a boat and a picnic lunch; you can soak in a flower bath and watch the boats come in from the spa suites at the Phuket Yacht Club.

shopping mall, housing chic home décor shops like Lamont Antiques & Contemporary and Cocoon. These outlets cater to the discerning tastes of the nearby hotel guests as well as island residents with new villas to furnish.

Phuket is also one of Asia's premier yachting destinations. Every December, during the week of the King's birthday, international yachting crowds flock here to compete in the King's Cup Regatta, the region's top yachting event. A royal representative attends the ceremonies. Prince Henrik of Denmark was a regular participant for many years.

Aside from fantastic yachting during the most beautiful weather of the year, the regatta is even better known as a major social event, with lavish beach parties hosted by different sponsors each night. In fact, some people don't even sail—they just come along for the parties and glamorous atmosphere.

These days, millionaires from Tokyo, Hong Kong, Singapore and Europe are all discovering a mix of good value and high style in fabulous Phuket. With a conveniently

international airport, plus international schools, hospitals, shopping malls and plenty of golf, a home in Phuket is increasingly attractive to many urban families.

Phuket is undoubtedly Thailand's wealthiest province, with tourism its main source of revenue. But it also takes great earnings from tin mining and rubber cultivation. In spite of its commercialised aspect, the island has a distinctive culture stemming from its time as a major trading port for people from the Middle East, India, Malaysia, China and Portugal, who ventured to Phuket and engaged in tin and rubber trading. The heritage of Chinese immigrant coconut and rubber barons, and Portuguese traders, is mirrored in the Sino-Portuguese architecture in Phuket town. Temples and mosques represent the Muslim and Buddhist populations.

a modern tropical island

The mainland to the northeast of Phuket is Phang-Nga province, eye-catchingly pretty with its stunning limestone cliffs, karst formations rising from the sea, and tranquil setting with white sand beaches. The best beaches are on the western Andaman seaside. Of these, Khao Lak beach is the up-and-coming area for new boutique hotels with chic and contemporary minimalist interiors. The area is also noted for its offer of many sea activities like snorkelling and diving.

krabi: an island-hopper's paradise

East of Phuket rests the province of Krabi, also famous for its beautiful limestone karst formations that create a mystical and romantic landscape. There is a coastline with over 150 islands, wonderful for exploring by sea-canoe, sea-kayak, or long-tail boat, and basking in the view. Centuries ago, this area was a favourite hideout for pirates because of the many islets and caves to hide in and store loot. A number of famous pirate caves have become sightseeing landmarks, not to be missed during boat trips.

There are two aspects to Krabi. Firstly, the mainland features beaches with hotels and some smaller boutique hotels, many of them located on the biggest and most

Centuries ago, this area was a favourite hideout for pirates...

beautiful beach on the mainland, Ao Nang. Then there is the Krabi peninsula, the most gorgeous part of this area, accessible only by boat from the mainland.

On the Krabi peninsula are located two of the area's most famous and inspiring beaches, Railay and Ao Phra Nang. The latter, not to be confused with Ao Nang on the mainland, is a stunning vision: a crescent of white sand ending with a spectacular limestone cliff on one end, with a tall karst formation jutting out of the water in the midst of the cove. During sundown, the golden light lends the cliff walls a brilliant orange glow, bathing the jagged limestone stalactites in magic.

In this cliff is a cave called Tham Phra Nang Nok or 'Outer Princess Cave'. Legend has it that in the 3rd century BC, an Indian princess drowned nearby when her boat capsized in a storm. It is believed that the princess' spirit inhabits this cave. Here, a picturesque shrine has been dedicated to her; it's surrounded by dozens of offerings of wooden fertility symbols from local fisher-folk to bring them luck in the sea's bounty.

From the outside, the cliff face looks like a solid mountain. But inside a surprise lies in wait—a lagoon named Sa Phra Nang. This can only be accessed by climbing up the exterior cliff wall and down into the interior with a rope. The trail up the cliff also has a vantage point that rewards your efforts with a gorgeous view of the two bays curving on each side. Hardy souls who manage to get to the top can feast their eyes on a fantastic overhead view of the entire peninsula.

Yet another recently discovered cave inside the cliff is Tham Phra Nang Nai or 'Inner Princess Cave', consisting of three stunning limestone caverns highlighted by a sparkling quartz wall, resembling a glittering waterfall. According to local lore, this cave is actually the grand palace of the legendary sea princess.

With all the stunning limestone cliffs in the area, it's no wonder that rock-climbing is the key sport here. The combination of picturesque cliffs and breathtaking scenery has turned the Krabi peninsula into a mecca for rock climbers from all around the world. There are a number of rock-climbing operations on the beach and a rock-climbing school as well, for those hoping to improve their skills.

The peninsula also has one beautiful luxury resort, numerous smaller bungalow types, and a compound of private villas owned by Bangkok residents, that can be rented. Many people staying on the mainland come here for day trips by long-tail boat. A number of sea-canoeing and sea-kayaking operations will take you happily paddling into the scenic waterways among the mangrove, and right into hidden lagoons and sea caves among the karst islets.

One of the most enjoyable activities in Krabi is taking boat trips to neighbouring islands like Koh Podah and Koh Gai or 'Chicken Island'—so called because it has a towering formation topped by a bulbous outcrop and its profile creates an irresistible imitation of a chicken's neck and head. Amidst these islands, you can snorkel among fish that swim bravely up to you and eat bread from your hand.

An up-and-coming district of Krabi province is Koh Lanta, a cluster of 52 islands. Here budget beach bungalows are making way for a handful of hip hotels like the chic Costa Lanta and SriLanta, each focusing on stylish seclusion on the biggest island, Koh Lanta Yai or 'Big Lanta Island'.

koh phi phi: a magical setting

Phi Phi is an area of two beautiful islands 40 km (25 miles) south of Krabi. They wore their astonishing beauty much better about two decades ago, before mass tourism took over. The larger of the two islands is Phi Phi Don, with two bays curving back to back to create a dumbbell shape. It is covered with bungalow resorts, cafés and restaurants.

The smaller island is Phi Phi Leh, which is uninhabitable because it consists of high, steep cliffs that drop straight into the sea. Phi Phi Leh is known for two lovely coves, Ao Maya and Lo Sama, both encircled by the high cliffs and pleasant for snorkelling. Ao Maya was the location for the filming of the Leonardo DiCaprio film *The Beach*, living proof that magical lagoons aren't the stuff of dreams; in Thailand they really do exist.

thailand's cleanest city

Further south of Krabi is Trang, which has even more lovely limestone cliffs and karst outcrops. However, being less frequented by travellers, it is more pristine. The city of Trang has a long history as an important trading post since the 1st century BC. During the time of the Indonesian Srivijaya empire, from the 7th to 12th centuries, Trang was a major commercial hub between this area and Malaysia.

Trang is regarded as Thailand's cleanest city, and likewise, the beach attracts nature lovers for its unmarred beauty. The Trang coast has several sandy beaches and coves with small, unpretentious resorts. A number of neighbouring islands are perfect for day trips. Koh Muk and Koh Kradan offer simple bungalow accommodation. Both are famed for having water so clear the sea floor can be clearly seen from your boat. An unusual enclosed green lagoon called Tham Morakot ('emerald cave') reposes in Koh Muk, and is reached only at low tide by boat via an 80 m (262 ft) limestone tunnel. A handful of smaller islands are also found in the area, all providing small coves, cosy beaches and corals reefs for snorkelling.

the similan islands

On the must-see list of all scuba diving enthusiasts, the Similan Islands are considered one of the top 10 dive sites of the world. The name comes from the Malay word for nine, sembilan, because there are nine islands in the archipelago. In Thai, each island has a number as well as a name. The islands are small and uninhabited because the archipelago is a national marine park. However, the attraction lies deeper: underneath the sea, clear waters result in visibility from 2 to 30 m (7 to 98 ft) among the troughs and sea walls. There are enough leopard sharks to delight nature lovers, and a sighting of the elusive and exotic whale shark can be a real treat.

The best diving season is December to May, and it can get very crowded during peak holidays like Christmas and the Thai New Year holidays in April. During those times, the most popular dive sites give the impression of being parking lots for boats!

THIS PAGE (FROM TOP): The further south you go in Thailand, the more pristine the beaches and deserted the islands will be; leopard sharks can be seen galore lazing around the sea bottom in the Similan Islands.

OPPOSITE: Thailand's southern islands are an international diving mecca.

...one of the top 10 dive sites of the world.

Dusit Resort, Hua Hin

THIS PAGE (FROM TOP): *Sweeping vistas of seas, sunset and impeccable landscaping; Hua Hin has an atmosphere of welcoming luxury.*

OPPOSITE: *Warm tones of ochre and red reflect traditional Thai influences in the contemporary yet classic guest suites.*

Just 2.5 hours from Bangkok, Hua Hin is the aristocrat of Thailand's beach resorts. On a beachfront overlooking the Gulf of Siam, this spectacular resort blends classic Thai hospitality and authentic charm with beautiful furnishings to deliver a unique holiday experience you won't forget.

The Dusit Resort, Hua Hin is home to 300 tastefully appointed rooms and suites, all with private balconies overlooking the sea or the surrounding lush, opulent gardens. Bathed in natural light, the contemporary rooms combine elements of natural woods and warm, textured silks. These luxurious amenities make guests feel right at home.

The Dusit Resort is an impressive venue for function and events, whatever the occasion. Well-equipped meeting and conference facilities make work a sheer pleasure. Or the magnificent ballroom can accommodate up to 1,000 people for a lavish banquet. Themed events are popular here too. From casual beach barbecues to a

...this spectacular resort blends classic Thai hospitality and authentic charm...

formal dinner at the nearby Summer Palace of King Rama VI, the Dusit Resort, Hua Hin always provides unsurpassed service. Guests come here confident that almost anything can be put together with enough notice—a testament to the resort's professionalism and passion for its business.

Within the hotel are dining options that leave guests spoiled for choice. The Coffee Shop and Brasserie has a casual ambience which is the perfect thing for long, lazy breakfasts and lunches, accompanied by the breathtaking view of the azure sea. It serves both international and Thai favourites that will satiate even the most discerning of palates. Meanwhile, Ban Benjarong, the resort's classic Thai restaurant does justice to its cuisine with its setting in a traditional-style Thai house, complete with sweeping roofs and ornately carved pillars. The food is equally amazing. Chefs balance the complex Thai flavours and presentation as if creating a work of art.

Adrenaline-pumping water sports, tennis courts, a state of the art gym and a whopping 1,500-sq m (16,146-sq ft) pool are all there for the taking.

And if decadent pleasures are more your thing, the resort's Devarana Spa offers a host of exquisite spa treatments to soothe and pamper. Otherwise, sit by the pristine beach and watch the day turn into night.

Unforgettable memories are made of these at the Dusit Resort, Hua Hin.

FACTS		
ROOMS	2 presidential suites • 7 executive suites • 26 landmark suites • 26 sea-facing rooms • 34 standard Lanai rooms • 205 standard rooms	
FOOD	The Brasserie: Thai and international • Ban Benjarong: Thai • San Marco: Italian • Rim Talay: international grill • Coffee Shop	
DRINK	polo bar • pool terrace • lobby lounge	
FEATURES	tennis and squash courts • pool • garden pool • gym • jacuzzi • water sports • horse riding • business centre • shopping arcade • beauty salon • spa • florist	
NEARBY	King Rama VI Summer Palace	
CONTACT	1349 Petchkasem Road, Cha-Am, Phetchaburi 76120 • telephone: +66.32.520 009/442 100 • facsimile: +66.32.520 296 • email: dcp@dusit.com • website: www.huahin.dusit.com	

PHOTOGRAPHS COURTESY OF DUSIT RESORT, HUA HIN.

Evason Hideaway + Six Senses Spa at Hua Hin

comforts envelop you in an oasis of rest and relaxation? Sun loungers allow guests to acquire their tans in private, while a pool in every villa offers a quiet dip.

Each sublimely comfortable bed is veiled by a sheath of soft netting to keep the few tropical insects at bay. Bath time is an elegant treat when taken outdoors in the sunken tub set in the villa's lotus pond or garden. And with plush daybeds so inviting, it is hard not to curl up in this Hideaway to escape from the world in the fantasy of a riveting book.

The Earth Spa by Six Senses is unlike any other spa. Constructed entirely from natural materials, it comprises a cluster of nine circular, domed buildings, in a

This is one resort that certainly lives up to its name. Tucked away in Pranburi, approximately 23 km (14 miles) south of Hua Hin and 230 km (143 miles) from Bangkok, Evason Hideaway & Six Senses Spa at Hua Hin consists of a collection of über contemporary villas, promising Thai-style tranquillity and privacy.

The cares of the outside world vanish as you enter its compound of sleek architecture and thoughtful design. All its villas—save for the sole Deluxe Pool Villa—come with a private spa option that includes a spa shower and steam room, a treatment area and fitness facilities on request. Why venture out of these villas when inside, all its

THIS PAGE (LEFT TO RIGHT): The sunken sala Living Room restaurant and bar exudes rustic charm; the Pool Villa Suite Master Bathroom mirrors the resort's chic, modern design.

OPPOSITE: The distinctively Thai Pool Villa Suite is a perfect place for unwinding.

gorgeous setting of water and landscaping. The treatment rooms, meditation cave and relaxation area literally seem to be floating on the ponds, caressed by gentle breezes.

If well-being counts as the sixth sense, then the spa scores full marks. Using its philosophy of "skin food", where only ingredients good enough to be eaten will be applied to your skin, a treatment here truly nourishes the mind, body and soul. Countless guests are drawn to this unique spa to awaken their sixth sense.

Dining at this Hideaway is also an experience not to be missed. A 24-hour in-villa dining menu means guests can eat what and when they want to. Romantic meals for two are the speciality here—champagne breakfast delivered on a beautiful tray to your terrace perhaps? Or maybe you'd prefer a barbecue in your private space, just for you and your partner. Even lunch takes on a romantic patina when enjoyed as a picnic on your front lawn.

PHOTOGRAPHS COURTESY OF EVASON HIDEAWAY + SIX SENSES SPA AT HUA HIN.

FACTS		
	ROOMS	55 pool villas and pool villa suites
	FOOD	The Beach Restaurant: Mediterranean • villa dining • The Living Room: Deli
	DRINK	The Bar • The Wine Cellar
	FEATURES	spa • tennis • water sports • trekking • nature trails
	NEARBY	Hua Hin
	CONTACT	9/22 Moo 5 Paknampran Beach, Pranburi, Prachuap Khiri Khan 77220 • telephone: +66.32.618 200 • facsimile: +66.32.618 201 • email: reservations-huahin@evasonhideaways.com • website: www.sixsenses.com/hideaway-huahin

Evason Hua Hin Resort + Six Senses Spa

There is something intensely pleasurable about sipping an ice-cold drink at The Bar on a tropical afternoon whilst gazing out across the sea, or dining al fresco beside shimmering lotus ponds at The Other Restaurant. These experiences spell holiday with a capital H at Evason Hua Hin Resort & Six Senses Spa. Situated 23 km (14 miles) away from Hua Hin, this collection of fresh, unconventional rooms and villas is the ideal escape from the everyday routine and stress of daily life.

The resort's 185 guestrooms are spread out within eight low-rise buildings set amidst a verdant tropical garden. 40 pool villas are hidden away within walled gardens with their own private plunge pools and outdoor sunken bathtubs. The Evason Studios feature unique outdoor terrace living options. Should guests prefer to sleep under the stars, a diaphanous canopy and mosquito net draped over a generous daybed are at their disposal for an al fresco slumber.

Nearby, mountain bike and hiking trails are the perfect activities for outdoor enthusiasts seeking adventure. Avid golfers can also play a round at any one of the six excellent golf courses that lie within a 30-minute drive of the resort. Water sports, tennis and even archery are available for those who fancy working up a bit of a sweat. But if it's holiday indulgence you're after, nothing quite beats several hours spent at the resort's Six Senses Spa.

Situated amongst lush vegetation and restful water features, the Six Senses Spa offers a host of treatments to help re-establish physical, mental and spiritual

...this collection of fresh, unconventional rooms and villas is the ideal escape...

THIS PAGE (FROM TOP): *The upper level of The Bar has an elegant atmosphere for relaxing; the poolside and impeccable service are a wonderful combination for restful days.*

OPPOSITE: *The pool villas are a welcome respite from the stress and grind of daily life.*

harmony. An extensive menu of services makes sure there is something for every individual, but if you can't decide, you won't go wrong with the Sensory Spa Journey.

The Journey begins with a luxurious footbath to calm before two massage therapists work to knead the stress out of your system. This experience is enhanced with a facial and scalp massage. Healthy spa cuisine is available at all the resort's well-designed restaurants.

But if decadence is the buzzword of your holiday, there is a host of delectable offerings, from classic Thai dishes to international and innovative fusion cuisine. Or request a picnic, and find a perfect spot to drink in the sun and admire breathtaking views of the Andaman Sea.

FACTS

ROOMS	145 rooms • 40 pool villas
FOOD	The Restaurant: International and Thai • The Other Restaurant: New Asian
DRINK	The Bar • The Wine Cellar • poolside
FEATURES	spa • pool • kid's club • fitness centre • boutique • library with Internet access • archery • tennis • sea sports • volleyball
NEARBY	hiking and mountain bike trails • golf courses • Hua Hin town
CONTACT	9 Moo 3 Paknampran Beach, Pranburi, Prachuap Khiri Khan, 77220 • telephone: +66.32.632 111 • facsimile: +66.32.632 112 • email: reservations-huahin@evasonresorts.com • website: www.sixsenses.com/evason-huahin

PHOTOGRAPHS COURTESY OF EVASON HUA HIN RESORT + SIX SENSES SPA.

Veranda Resort + Spa

Just a two-hour drive from Bangkok, the resort town of Hua Hin is a world away from the traffic and noise. Tranquil and wonderfully rustic, it has served as a popular getaway for the residents of Thailand's bustling capital since the 1920s. Today, Hua Hin still retains its quiet charm and provincial flavour, partly because it is the country's Royal playground where the King has taken up residence in his golden years.

Amidst Hua Hin's pristine coastline, with crystalline beaches straight out of a picture postcard, sits the Veranda Resort and Spa. A dream location for an indulgent break. Here, sunrises are simply magnificent to behold and sunsets are contemplative in their beauty—especially when viewed from the plush balconies of its spacious rooms, villas and suites, with a glass of fine wine and the company of someone special.

No resort is complete without delicious fare to tempt and delight its hungry guests. When hunger pangs strike, the resort's Dining Room comes to the rescue every time. Open all day, the restaurant serves a pleasing and mouth-watering array of Western, Thai and fusion dishes that will satiate even the heartiest of appetites. Meanwhile, Veranda's second restaurant, Rabiang Lay, dishes up amazing seafood creations right by the beach. Sink your toes into the perfect white sand as you sink your teeth into delicious treats like crispy prawn pancakes and sea scallops in golden bags. And by night, bask in the soft glow of candlelight and moonlight as everything around you takes on a romantic patina. Life should always be this good.

FACTS

ROOMS	72 rooms • 2 executive suites • 10 pool villas • 3 beachfront villas
FOOD	The Dining Room: Western, Thai and fusion • Rabiang Lay: seafood
DRINK	Lobby Lounge
FEATURES	spa • pool • fitness centre • Internet room • kids' club • meeting and conference facilities
NEARBY	Bangkok city
CONTACT	737/12 Mung Talay Road Cha Am, 76120 Phetchaburi • telephone (office): +66.22.164 872/3 • telephone (resort): +66.32.709 000-99 • facsimile: +66.26.116 710 • email: rsvn@verandaresortandspa.com • website: www.verandaresortandspa.com

PHOTOGRAPHS COURTESY OF VERANDA RESORT + SPA.

Dusit Resort, Pattaya

Set on its own private beach at the exclusive northern end of Thailand's Pattaya Bay, the Dusit Resort, Pattaya offers the best the city has to offer. Secluded from the throng of the city, yet only a stone's throw away from it, Dusit Resort combines the languor of a beach resort with the delights of city-living convenience.

Enter its well-lit lobby and a sense of opulence and spaciousness greets you. Verdant tropical greenery combines with a palette of light shades to render a classic décor that is refreshingly upbeat. In its stylishly appointed rooms and suites, contemporary design and state-of-the-art amenities meet. Sit at your own scenic balcony and gaze at the panoramic ocean vista or at the lavish emerald garden view. Coupled with the Dusit Resort's renowned hospitality, a stay in any one of these rooms is an experience to savour.

To keep guests entertained and satiated, an impressive selection of wining and dining venues are available. At the top

THIS PAGE (FROM TOP): *Relax in the lobby where colours reflect the tropical sunshine; blissful sea views from the uniquely landscaped pool.*

OPPOSITE (FROM LEFT): *Verdant greenery offers a retreat from the bustle of city life; The Bay Restaurant serves sumptuous Italian cuisine.*

of the list is The Peak, which is widely known as the finest and most stylish Chinese restaurant in Pattaya. Serving both Cantonese and other regional Chinese cuisine, meals here are healthy, served individually plated, presented Western-style, and are certainly memorable on the palate.

At The Bay, meals are a spectacular experience with enchanting views of Pattaya Bay. Alternatively, snuggle up in what the restaurant terms "lovers' nooks"—secluded pockets of space for intimate dining. Under the watchful eye of executive chef Maurizio Menconi, The Bay serves a splendid menu,

with a concept based on four strict principles: use imports from Italy only; mix them with top grade local ingredients; prepare dishes based on authentic northern Italian recipes; and present all creations with a modern twist. Indeed, it is a recipe for success, evident at first bite of any one of The Bay's dishes.

For an adrenaline rush, head to the beach where facilities for diving, sailing and boating await. The resort boasts a fitness studio, an aerobics studio, steam room, sauna and sports bars. For a spot of pampering, head to the resort's Devarana Spa. Inspired by a legendary garden in heaven, the spa offers exquisite treatments performed by skilled therapists. Only natural products that contain herbal preparations and the freshest ingredients are used.

By night, wander off to the nearby shopping areas and soak up the vibrant atmosphere before returning to your Dusit Resort, Pattaya suite for a blissful slumber.

FACTS

ROOMS	287 superior rooms • 20 suites • 89 club rooms • 24 deluxe rooms • 42 grand rooms •
FOOD	Cascade Café: international • The Bay: Italian • The Peak: Chinese • Seafood BBQ Terrace
DRINK	Lobby Lounge
FEATURES	Devarana Spa • Dusit Shop • Dusit Resort Sports Club • pools • watersports • tennis courts • Napalai Convention Hall • business centre • shopping gallery
NEARBY	golf • diving • Pattaya City Hall • Pattaya Centre
CONTACT	240/2 Pattaya Beach Road, Pattaya City, Chonburi • telephone: +66.38.425 611-7 • facsimile: +66.38.428 239 • email: pattaya@dusit.com • website: www.dusit.com

Amari Emerald Cove Resort

THIS PAGE (FROM TOP): *Set in a national park, the resort affords idyllic views of the sea and pristine white sand beach; the low-rise resort with classic Thai accents; relax by the pool.*

OPPOSITE: *Spacious and elegant guest rooms are rich in teak, soft in colour schemes, contrasting with the lush greenery outside.*

Recently developed on Thailand's second largest island, Koh Chang, the Amari Emerald Cove Resort's idyllic charms beckon. Although it is second in size only to Phuket, Koh Chang has escaped large-scale development that has overtaken much of Thailand's other jewel-like islands.

Koh Chang forms part of a national park, and its natural beauty is fittingly geared for quieter pursuits—the only speedboats you see are those used to ferry excursions to nearby islands. Koh Chang's spectacular sea sights are best viewed underwater, where visibility can reach up to 30 m (98 ft) during the best diving months of October to the end of May.

Being on its own stretch of sandy beach on the west coast of Koh Chang, the Amari Emerald Cove Resort blends harmoniously into the natural environment. Just a short drive and ferry-ride away from the newly opened Trat airport, this new resort destination features 165 large, comfortable rooms decorated in contemporary Asian style. Smooth teak floors, local stone bathroom fixtures and Thai-themed furnishings evoke a sense of oriental calm. All superior and deluxe rooms measure a spacious 40 sq m (431 sq ft) and come with their own terrace that overlooks the cerulean sea or the resort's well-tended gardens. This is the resort where you can take it as easy or be as active as you want. Within its grounds is everything you need to hide away from the world—a palm-shaded swimming pool, a spa, restaurants and a fabulous beach.

Outside are a myriad of sights and activities that could keep you busy for weeks. Dive the wreck of the Thonburi, which sank in 1921; or snorkel near Bird Island where the countless corals are as vivid as a technicolour movie. Scenic hiking trails, elephant treks and numerous waterfalls are but a short jaunt away. And full-day tours around the island offer the unbeatable experience of visiting Koh Chang's ancient temples and sleepy fishing villages.

When you return to the resort, unwind at the Poolbar located next to the sprawling 50 m (1,969 ft) pool. This is the ideal place to kick back and sip a cocktail. Next, head to any one of the resort's three restaurants for a satisfying meal of international, Thai or Italian delights. Amari Emerald Cove is a gem of a holiday destination.

PHOTOGRAPHS COURTESY OF AMARI EMERALD COVE RESORT.

FACTS		
ROOMS	7 suites • 81 deluxe rooms • 77 superior rooms	
FOOD	Cove Terrace: International • Just Thai: Thai • Sassi: Italian	
DRINK	Poolbar • Breezes Lounge	
FEATURES	spa • activities centre • fitness room • babysitting • banquet facilities • Internet access • tailor shop • drug store • dive centre	
NEARBY	Koh Rang Pinnacles • Koh Lao Ya Nok (Bird Island) • elephant treks • Koh Lao Ya Nai (wreck dive) • hiking trails • Than Mayom Waterfall	
CONTACT	88/8 Moo 4, Tambol Koh Chang, King Amphur, Koh Chang 23170 • telephone: +66.39.552 000 • facsimile: +66.39.552 001 • email: emeraldcove@amari.com • website: www.amari.com	

Anantara Resort + Spa Koh Samui

Overlooking the azure waters and white-sand beaches of Bophut Bay is the Anantara Resort and Spa Koh Samui. This member of Small Luxury Hotels is set on 4.5 hectares (11 acres) of beachfront, next to the haven of Fisherman's Village. Less than 10 minutes away from the airport by car, this boutique-sized resort is a world unto itself. With hip, minimalist interiors, the Anantara Koh Samui is the most gorgeous escape on this holiday island awash in sunlight and cooled by gentle sea breezes.

Throughout the resort, southern Thai architecture and motifs abound. Geometric gingerbread fretwork, batik fabrics and warm shades of red and ochre all conspire to evoke a sense of old-meets-new Oriental charm. Add to that dove cages, wind bells and wide open spaces, and you get a hideaway of your dreams.

While days are best spent lazing by the 30 m (98 ft) infinity-edge pool, nights are made for romantic relaxation in Anantara's signature made-for-two terrazzo bathtubs, the focal point of every room. Set in a low-rise, horseshoe-shaped building, all guestrooms and suites feature a spacious balcony and their own in-room pets: a trio of beautiful Siamese fighting fish.

To keep guests connected, wireless high-speed Internet access is available in the resort's library, lobby, restaurants and suites.

Also available are Thai cooking classes, a 130-capacity ballroom for special events, and a host of water sports.

The inspiring Anantara Spa has private suites and pavilions set in their own walled courtyard, while three ethereal treatment suites are encased in glass. Enjoy sublime treatments like Ayurvedic massage therapies, skin enhancement treatments, and a sun soother—relief for your sun-kissed skin.

Meals at Anantara are also sensuous affairs. The resort's Full Moon Italian

THIS PAGE (FROM TOP): Traditional mixed with modern—the pool with Thai sculptures; al fresco dining in a sala.

OPPOSITE (FROM LEFT): The spacious lobby and rooms are rich in woods and natural tones; rejuvenate at the Anantara Spa.

...the most gorgeous escape on this holiday island...

restaurant is cleverly cantilevered over the edge of the swimming pool, offering diners the sensation of hovering between a dramatic torch-lit waterway and the deep blue sea. Its three interlocking terraces begin with the pool bar on the lowest level and are elevated to two floors of dining. All of these are illuminated by a full moon globe, suspended from the ceiling, highlighting polished concrete beams as well as the teak and copper-trimmed furniture. Fittingly, the food here is equally magnificent.

PHOTOGRAPHS COURTESY OF ANANTARA RESORT + SPA KOH SAMUI.

FACTS

ROOMS	6 royal suites • 18 suites • 30 deluxe terraces • 52 deluxe rooms
FOOD	Full Moon Italian Restaurant: Italian • High Tide: Thai
DRINK	Pool Bar • Eclipse Bar
FEATURES	spa • pool • tennis courts • fitness centre • ballroom • Thai cooking classes • children's club • water sports
NEARBY	Fisherman's Village
CONTACT	99/9 Moo 1 Bo Phut Bay, Koh Samui, Surat Thani 84320 • telephone: +66.77.428 300 • facsimile: +66.77.428 310 • email: infosamui@anantara.com • website: www.anantara.com

SALA Samui Resort + Spa

First impressions of SALA Samui Resort and Spa are of a tasteful, upmarket neighbourhood, with homes so beautifully appointed, you'll want to stay longer. This five-star pool villa resort is one of Koh Samui's most stylish offerings.

Combining traditional Thai architecture with modern contemporary facilities and amenities, SALA Samui is all about peaceful, personal space blessed with impeccable design and landscaping.

There are seven different varieties of accommodation available here—deluxe balcony rooms, garden pool villas, signature SALA pool villas, one- and two-bedroom suites and the palatial beachfront presidential pool villa. Whichever you choose to stay in, personalised, intimate service is a guarantee.

Of its 69 villas, 53 boast private swimming pools which hint at lazy days of frolicking in the tropical sun. When the heat

THIS PAGE (FROM TOP): Dine at the scenic SALA Samui Restaurant; garden pavilions, water features and a courtyard embrace tranquillity around the beachfront lap pool.

OPPOSITE: Tastefully decorated villas offer sumptuous bedrooms (left), open air baths (centre) and dining area (right).

...SALA Samui is all about peaceful, personal space...

gets too much, retreat to the cream and wood rich villa, on oversized outdoor daybeds with a good book.

The air-conditioned villas, with their rich vanilla fabrics and cool bamboo accents are constantly bathed in natural light. Open-air bathrooms with lovely bathtubs and outdoor rain showers are surrounded by lush and colourful tropical gardens.

SALA Samui's location on Choeng Mon Beach is an ideal base from which to explore this beautiful Thai island. Within a five-minute distance is Samui airport as well as Bophut's quaint Fisherman's Village. 10 minutes away is the shopping strip and nightlife of Chaweng Beach.

For added indulgence head for the Mandara Spa. Blended into the lush landscape with garden pavilions and courtyards, the spa is a hideaway unto itself. Tranquil sounds of rippling water and the aromas of natural herbs and spices soothe.

Mealtimes at SALA Samui are equally special. At the SALA Samui Restaurant, exquisite choices abound—succulent steaks, fresh daily seafood, classic pasta dishes, or spicy Thai offerings.

Of course, guests can choose to dine privately in their villas, where delicious meals could lead to other delicious activities.

SALA's extensive wine cellar will also help lubricate a starry night of unbridled decadence and enchantment.

FACTS

ROOMS	16 deluxe balcony rooms • 16 garden pool villas • 28 SALA pool villas • 4 one-bedroom pool villa suites • 2 one-bedroom duplex pool villa suites • 2 two-bedroom pool villa suites • 1 two-bedroom presidential pool villa suite
FOOD	SALA Samui Restaurant: Thai and international
DRINK	SALA Samui Wine Cellar • Beach Bar
FEATURES	2 beachfront swimming pools • Mandara Spa • cooking classes • gift shop • library with complimentary Internet connection • boardroom
NEARBY	Samui airport • Fisherman's Village • Chaweng Beach
CONTACT	10/9 Moo 5, Baan Plai Laem, Bophut, Koh Samui, Suratthani 84320 • telephone: +66.77.245 888 • facsimile: +66.77.245 889 • email: info@salasamui.com • website: www.salasamui.com

PHOTOGRAPHS COURTESY OF SALA SAMUI RESORT + SPA.

Sila Evason Hideaway + Spa at Samui

Sila Evason Hideaway & Spa at Samui has often been credited with setting new standards of excellence in Thailand's five-star resorts. A study in modern contemporary luxury, the Hideaway is aptly named.

Perched on a headland on the northern tip of Koh Samui, Sila Evason Hideaway is nestled among 8 hectares (20 acres) of indigenous plants. The resort offers stunning views of the Gulf of Siam and the outlying islands. Within these surrounds are 66 uniquely designed villas that cocoon guests in their own world of sheer luxury, pampering and serenity. Most of the split-level villas come with private sundecks and infinity-edge pools—guests can feel like the only person in the entire resort.

Each villa is clad in sleek timber panels, cool terrazzo and rich fabrics. As befits a sumptuous resort, there are well-trained butlers who will tend to your every need. And for deep relaxation, the Hideaway Spa, with its open-air rooms and professional therapists, provides 'high touch'

treatments that focus on de-stressing the mind and body. Choose from a menu that includes massages, body scrubs and wraps, fragrant baths, and beauty treatments. You can also indulge in holistic therapies such as hypnotherapy and even life-coaching. You will leave the spa radiating well-being.

When your body and mind have been rejuvenated at the spa, partake of the exquisite dining experience that all Evason Hideaways have become famous for. With an emphasis on only the finest, freshest ingredients in every dish, food at this Hideaway constitutes a sublime experience.

Dining On The Hill, the resort's central restaurant, serves tempting international fare and local specialties. Choose your favourite wines from Drinks On The Hill, the resort's extensive cellar, featuring labels from the world's most respected wine regions. Then gaze out at the magnificent night view as you sink back with a satisfied palate onto comfortable oversized chairs.

Or savour aperitifs at the bar, Drinks On The Rocks, with a 270-degree view of the sea, followed by an elegant dinner of New Asian cuisine at Dining On The Rocks.

As the rays of the setting sun weave shadows in the bar, you will have found your own little slice of paradise.

THIS PAGE: Pool villas are graced by superb views of the sea.

OPPOSITE (FROM TOP): Dining on the Hill with its eclectic fare, will be unforgettable; a pool villa bedroom with its soothing vistas is where you can forget all your worries.

FACTS		
ROOMS	14 hideaway villas • 41 pool villas • 10 pool villa suites • 1 presidential villa
FOOD	Dining On The Hill: Thai and modern Mediterranean • Dining On The Rocks: New Asian and international • villa dining
DRINK	Drinks On The Hill • Drinks On The Rocks
FEATURES	spa • pool • water sports centre • Six Senses gallery • gym • boardroom
NEARBY	Big Buddha • 18-hole golf course
CONTACT	9/10 Moo, Baan Plai Laem, Bophut, Koh Samui, Suratthani 84320 • telephone: +66.77.245 678 • facsimile: +66.77.245 671 • email: reservations-samui@evasonhideaways.com • website: www.sixsenses.com/hideaway-samui

The Sarojin

It is evident that The Sarojin takes its hospitality seriously. After all, it was named after a mythical lady, the daughter of a prominent Thai nobleman, who was regarded as the perfect host. To be sure, the resort sits in a lush tropical garden setting and feels much like a friend's plush private estate in the beautiful area of Khao Lak in Phang Nga. Here, rich forests and the world-class underwater pleasures of the Similan Islands are an invitation to kick back, relax and enjoy luxury at its very best.

At the heart of The Sarojin is a giant old ficus tree, a magnificent split-level lotus pond and gurgling natural stream. Surrounded by this bounty of nature spread across 4 hectares (10 acres), The Sarojin is all about space. The Sarojin features 56 contemporary Asian-inspired residences, and private access to a stunning-white beach fringing the warm Andaman Sea. Couples' baths and waterfall showers show off The Sarojin's sensual side, while regular suites feature sala sundecks. A 25-m (82-ft) infinity-edged swimming pool and a large jacuzzi provide further aquatic indulgence.

If you dream of sailing away into the sunset, The Sarojin has its own 12 m (38 ft) luxury boat for exclusive use by its guests. Or if you'd like to get out to explore other places, your hosts at the Sarojin can tailor personalised excursions to suit every taste.

Well-being takes on a special significance here. The Pathways spa, hidden from view by mangroves, sits over the central energy lay line of The Sarojin, sending out positive, healing vibes to all who visit. The ancient and sacred come together, highlighted with modern touches of comfort to awaken and relax.

The Sarojin approach to eating is gorgeously organic. Expect fresh new tastes and plenty of originality. Dine under the hanging roots of the ficus tree, where a delectable menu of international gourmet cuisine is served daily. Adjacent to it is the Cellar, an al fresco long bar stocked with the best international wine labels. Otherwise, dine under the sky at The Edge, a beachside restaurant serving fresh seafood straight from the Andaman Sea. But if true beachfront dining is what you're after, head to the silken beach with a gourmet picnic basket and a bottle of Chilean white. Then wind down at The Sarojin Lounge, just above the lotus pond.

PHOTOGRAPHS COURTESY OF THE SAROJIN.

FACTS		
ROOMS	56 guest residences: 14 Sarojin suites • 14 pool residences • 28 garden residences	
FOOD	Ficus • The Edge • in residence dining	
DRINK	The Sarojin Lounge • The Cellar	
FEATURES	spa • fitness centre • croquet lawn • pétanque (boules) • water sports • library • luxury 12 m (38 ft) boat • mountain bikes	
NEARBY	Similan Island National Marine Park • Khao Lak and Khao Sok National Parks • Blue Canyon Country Club • Surin Islands National Marine Park • diving	
CONTACT	60 Moo 2, Kukkak, Takupa, Phang Nga • telephone: +66.76.427 900 • facsimile: +66.76.427 906 • email: info@sarojin.com • website: www.sarojin.com	

The Paradise Koh Yao Beach Resort + Spa

To regular guests of this boutique beach resort, it is simply known as Paradise—an apt name for a luxury hideaway on a stretch of pristine, private beach that has served as a backdrop for movies like *The Beach* and *The Man With The Golden Gun*.

Situated on Koh Yao Island, The Paradise Koh Yao Boutique Beach Resort and Spa doesn't just offer a getaway from the rigours of city living. It aims to reconnect its guests with the great outdoors and restore the pleasures of breathing in fresh, unpolluted air. Indeed, it is easy to feel completely at one with nature here. The Paradise was designed to harmonise with its environment and all the existing trees and plants. Even the abandoned rice paddies of the surrounding areas were incorporated into its landscape features.

Barely visible from the sea, The Paradise's cluster of whitewashed thatched villas is perched on the beach between coconut palms and tamarind trees. From here, superb views of the sparkling sea flanked by majestic limestone cliffs are best enjoyed from your private villa pool or

THIS PAGE (FROM TOP): Idyllic sea views from a beach hammock; the elegant Pool Villa opens out to nature and the sea.

OPPOSITE (FROM LEFT): Relax with a cocktail at the pool; or in your own Pool Villa; the indigenous-style spa sala is perfect for a massage amidst balmy breezes.

tropical garden. Behind the beach, a collection of luxurious studios have hillside jungle settings, and each sports its own outdoor jacuzzi over the deep blue bay.

Inside, the natural theme continues with stone floors, roughcast walls and dreamy king beds draped in cotton muslin netting. All bathrooms are indoor-outdoor affairs, allowing guests to shower 'outside' with a quick slide back of the partition doors.

Meals can be enjoyed under a canopy of shady trees at The Seafood Grill, a restaurant on the beach serving sensational international cuisine, with a selection of Thai favourites, grilled seafood and light dishes. A recent addition, The Al Fresco Restaurant attracts guests with its contemporary Mediterranean cuisine and authentic wood-fired oven pizzas.

After treating their taste buds to irresistible flavours, guests can retire to the resort's infinity-edge pool to lounge around, or venture out to explore the natural wonders of Phang Nga Bay. Despite its discovery by a 19th-century traveller, the bay remains one of the world's best-kept secrets, a wonderland full of indigenous plant and animal life. Tours and excursions to Phang Nga Bay can easily be organised by The Paradise, so guests won't miss out on the many activities, from private tours of the nearby trails and caves to guided jungle treks and mountain bike rides.

Upon your return, there's the Paradise Spa with natural herbal treatments to inject a new sense of relaxation into your being.

FACTS

ROOMS	48 superior studios • 16 deluxe studios with outdoor jacuzzi • 6 pool villas
FOOD	The Seafood Grill: Thai, international • The Al Fresco: Mediterranean
DRINK	beach bar
FEATURES	spa • pool • excursions • resort transfer boat • Internet access
NEARBY	Phang Nga Bay • Krabi • Phuket
CONTACT	24 Moo 4, Tambol Koh Yao Noi, Amphur Koh Yao, Phang Nga 82160 • telephone: +66.1.892 4878 • facsimile: +66.76.238 913• email: info@theparadise.biz • website: www.theparadise.biz

PHOTOGRAPHS COURTESY OF THE PARADISE KOH YAO BEACH RESORT + SPA.

Banyan Tree Phuket

Once they check in, guests of the Banyan Tree Phuket tend to take quite a while before they venture out of their villas; and it's no wonder. This sanctuary of the senses cradles guests in a dreamy escape, where silk-sheeted beds float on the edge of lily ponds and outdoor baths are filled with water cascading from gorgeous stone statues.

Every villa, from the Deluxe Villa to the Presidential Spa Pool Villa, is hidden within its own tropical garden. Each of these private universes, outfitted in sumptuous Thai silks and rich, dark woods, are furnished with all the requirements for decadent living. A bottle of bubbly, a gourmet meal, massage oils, candles—it's all been carefully thought through; your Banyan Tree Phuket villa is a veritable nesting place.

Open the bedroom doors and step out onto your very own spacious garden landscape, complete with raised sala pavilion and day beds, a sunken bath and a 27 sq m (291 sq ft) lap pool—do whatever you please away from prying eyes.

THIS PAGE (FROM LEFT): Enjoy a tranquil meal on the Sanya Rak dinner cruise; the Spa Pool Villa looks out upon your own private space with distinctive Thai style.

OPPOSITE (FROM LEFT): Luxurious Thai silks and rich woods lend decadence in the Spa Pool Villa; Saffron restaurant specialises in Asian and Thai fare.

...where silk-sheeted beds float on the edge of lily ponds...

It seems that resort heaven has never looked this good. Outside, the grounds of Banyan Tree Phuket are equally breathtaking. Picture-perfect amongst this sanctuary are 151 villas—with wat-styled roofs poking elegantly through the canopy.

Visiting Banyan Tree Phuket without visiting its award-winning Banyan Tree Spa would be like travelling to Cairo and missing the pyramids. It is here that the resort's well-trained therapists begin their magic, working their gentle yet strong fingers over your body to rejuvenate, energise and restore. Based on traditional Eastern philosophies, therapies utilise only the best of natural and local ingredients, such as sandalwood, kaffir lime and honey.

But if you dread venturing out of your villa to make the trip via buggy to the spa, then, of course, the spa will come to you. Ask for the Harmony Banyan Massage and not one but two therapists will arrive at your villa to simultaneously knead away your tension.

The beautiful Andaman Sea is only a short stroll away. Watch the sun make a quiet show of disppearance beneath the horizon as you sip an aperitif at the resort's Sand Bar. Enjoy dinner at one of the resort's elegant restaurants, or in the comfort of your personal villa. Alternatively, indulge in a romantic dinner on board Banyan Tree's traditional long-tail boat, The Sanya Rak (Promise of Love). Exquisite memories are made of these—at the Banyan Tree Phuket.

PHOTOGRAPHS COURTESY OF BANYAN TREE PHUKET.

FACTS

ROOMS	151 villas
FOOD	Saffron: Thai and Southeast Asian • Tamarind Restaurant: Western and Far Eastern • Watercourt: Mediterranean • Banyan Café: international • Sanya Rak Dinner Cruise • Sands: Barbecue lunch • In-villa dining
DRINK	pool bar • lobby bar • Sands Restaurant
FEATURES	Banyan Tree Spa • pool • tennis • yoga • meditation classes
NEARBY	Laguna Phuket Golf Club • Phi Phi Islands • Similan Islands • canoeing • Phang Nga Bay scuba diving • windsurfing
CONTACT	33 Moo 4 Srisoothorn Road, Cherngtalay, Amphur Talang, Phuket 83110 • telephone: +66.76.324 374 • facsimile: +66.76.324 375 • email: phuket@banyantree.com • website: www.banyantree.com

Evason Phuket Resort + Six Senses Spa

Among 26 hectares (64 acres) of landscaped tropical gardens, facing the sapphire Andaman Sea, is a cluster of 260 stylishly appointed suites and pool villas dispersed across five low-rise buildings. This is Evason Phuket Resort & Six Senses Spa. Just 25 minutes away from Phuket town, this haven of good taste has drawn guests from all over the world with its modern charms and superb service.

The majority of its gorgeous guest accommodations face the sea. The rest overlook the bay and coastline of verdant greenery. A honeymoon villa tucked away on Bon Island is a private slice of paradise all by itself. 15 minutes away by boat, Bon Island boasts a private beach with its own restaurant that opens only for lunch. Dinner at the honeymoon villa is often enjoyed indoors or under the starry night sky. Indeed, this exclusive retreat seems to have been perfectly made just for two.

A range of other delightful dining options await the resort's guests. Its main restaurant, Into The View, serves an irresistible Western and Asian breakfast buffet and a selection of international dishes in its à la carte menu. Dinnertime brings back the buffet, with different cuisine themes, from Asian to European. Into Thai, a sea-view restaurant offering specialties from Thailand's various regions, boasts an enticing walk-in wine cellar where guests are spoilt for choice. As you dine, a group of

THIS PAGE (FROM TOP): Dining promises to be special at Into The View Restaurant; chic elegance of the Duplex Pool Suite Bedroom; the Pool Villa inspires rest and relaxation.
OPPOSITE: The sleek exterior of the reception sala reflects the resort's tranquillity.

musicians add that special touch to your meal with lively performances. The talk of the island is Into Fusion, yet another restaurant that offers innovative dishes inspired by a delightful meeting of East and West. It has a spectacular list of over 300 wines from around the world to pair with your delicious meal.

The resort includes the Six Senses Spa, where you can indulge in soothing treatments and therapies—perfect for relaxation and recuperation.

You can also enjoy an invigorating game of volleyball or tennis, or go scuba diving in the nearby waters teeming with a fantastic array of fish and corals. Or go

island-hopping to see Phuket's enchanting neighbouring islands. As night falls, sip cocktails at the resort's lobby lounge or beach bar, or head out to Patong Beach—Phuket's centre of nightlife. All these activities might take you away from your room. But why venture out? Either way you'll have a great time.

FACTS		
	ROOMS	1 honeymoon suite • 259 rooms
	FOOD	Into The View: international • Into Thai: Thai • Into Fusion: international • Into The Beach: Mediterranean and wood-fired oven
	DRINK	lobby lounge • beach bar • pool bar
	FEATURES	spa • tennis • volleyball • kid's club • market visits • fitness centre • dive shop • boutique • library with Internet access
	NEARBY	Patong Beach • Phuket town
	CONTACT	100 Vised Road, Moo 2, Tambol Rawai, Muang District, Phuket 83100 • telephone: +66.76.381 010 • facsimile: +66.76.381 018 • email: reservations-phuket@evasonresorts.com • website: www.sixsenses.com/evason-phuket

PHOTOGRAPHS COURTESY OF EVASON PHUKET RESORT + SIX SENSES SPA.

Trisara

Barely 15 minutes from Phuket International Airport hides Trisara, Thailand's newest resort jewel. A Sanskrit word, Trisara means 'third garden in heaven', an apt name for a haven set amid a lush rainforest thick with bamboo and banana trees. This beautiful six-star resort was created by Anthony Lark, the young, erstwhile general manager of Amanpuri, which opened its doors 16 years ago. With Lark at the helm, Amanpuri quickly found its place at the top of 'must visit' lists for discerning, affluent travellers around the world.

Now, using the same winning formula of genuine hospitality, luxurious surroundings and brilliant design, combined with his passionate drive and dedication, Lark's Trisara has set the global benchmark for ultra luxurious tropical resorts once more. This remarkable achievement received prestigious acclaim just six months after opening in 2004, when Trisara was named 'Best of the Best' in the Robb Report 2005 annual survey (worldwide resort category).

With such pedigree, Trisara's guests can expect nothing less than the ultimate in enlightened and pampering resort experiences. Hidden along the quiet and largely undeveloped northwestern coastline of Thailand, Trisara sits over a private bay. The entire resort embodies back-to-nature luxury, albeit swishly redefined.

There are 24 individual pool villas, each with commanding ocean views, a breathtaking 10 m infinity-edge pool and a private outdoor shower courtyard. 18 new ocean-view pool suites bring the total number of Trisara resort villas to 42. These new rooms, each blessed with expansive sea views, comprise exquisite suites with outdoor showers, teak pool decks and a private pool. Indeed, such slices of unbridled privacy seem to deliciously hint at gloriously naked days and nights, where the outside world is a mere memory and where time moves at a languorous pace.

Trisara's rooms are elegantly relaxed and sexy. Resort chic goes sensual with touches of muted sand and stone shades, highlighted with hints of precious gold.

Acoustic considerations have also been stylishly planned—respectful space between each villa, opulent greenery and silent air-conditioning ensure that the only thing you'll hear is the blissful lap of the ocean and the trill of the forest that surrounds you. Of course, if you need to stay connected to the world outside, each villa is equipped with high-speed Internet access, a plasma TV, DVD player and surround-sound stereo.

A 45 m lap pool and a gym are there for the pleasure of all guests at Trisara, as is the beachfront restaurant. Don't miss the delectable speciality dishes—the sweet yellow-bean dumplings with sesame seeds and the banana-blossom salad with chicken and shrimp are sure to delight the most expert of tastebuds.

THIS PAGE: *Each private villa has its own infinity-edge pool.*
OPPOSITE: *With an absolute privacy policy, Trisara staff will leave you to soak up the sheer indulgences of your private hideaway, whilst remaining at your beck and call.*

Trisara's signature is unobtrusive service. If you want to be left alone, this is the place to go for restful relaxation. An absolute privacy policy means you'll enjoy a peaceful stay completely undisturbed by traditional service techniques. The staff to guest ratio is seven to one and they all know exactly how to leave you alone. Fancy dinner by your villa's poolside? The impeccably trained staff will magically arrange it and then quietly leave you to enjoy dining in blissful privacy. Conversely, should you ever need attention, Trisara's staff are there in a flash to turn your requests into action. This unique balance of leaving you alone whilst attending to your every need makes a stay at Trisara relaxing, special and unemcumbered by the comings and goings of day-to-day life.

THIS PAGE (FROM TOP): **One of Trisara's elegant and sumptuous villa bedrooms; dazzling views of the pristine ocean and private bay.**
OPPOSITE: **Savour the delicious privacy of your very own hideaway retreat.**

Guests mixing business with pleasure will appreciate Trisara's recently added meeting facilities, which encompass a new seafront meeting room, complete with state-of-the-art audiovisual equipment that includes an eight-channel mixing desk and a Bose speaker system. Business meetings or conferences will never be the same again, as this private room is perched directly above the sea in Trisara's own private bay. The room is surrounded by glass-walled sliding doors that open easily to drench the room in gorgeous natural light. So beautiful are the sea views revealed by the world outside, they may prove just that much too distracting for a corporate discussion.

If you want to be left alone, this is the place to go for restful relaxation.

If you're up for a spot of the outdoors, it is very easy to charter a luxury yacht and explore the deep blue around you. Trisara's neighbouring islands are perfect little gems for you to discover, with excellent diving or snorkelling opportunities that should not be missed. Also within striking distance are two world-class golf courses, the Blue Canyon and Laguna Golf Club, where avid golfers can enjoy a day honing their skills in gorgeous and exclusive surroundings. Alternatively, you can just take it all in from the comfort of your teakwood deckchair as you unwind, sipping a cocktail or two and contemplating the beauty all around you.

And if you find you may just like to stay at Trisara forever, there are the residential villas for rent or for sale. Lying adjacent to the resort, they are available in two- to five-bedroom configurations with 20 m (65.5 ft) private pools, live-in maids and chefs. A charmed life indeed for those who simply cannot leave the wonder of Trisara behind.

PHOTOGRAPHS COURTESY OF TRISARA.

FACTS		
	ROOMS	42 individual sea-facing pool villas and suites
	FOOD	private dining • poolside
	DRINK	bar
	FEATURES	luxury yachting • gym • tennis • beach • pool • diving • library • spa • salon
	NEARBY	Blue Canyon Golf Club
	CONTACT	60/1 Moo 6, Srisoonthorn Road, Cherngtalay, Talang, Phuket • telephone: +66.76.310 100 • facsimile: +66.76.310 300 • email: reservations@trisara.com • website: www.trisara.com

Twinpalms Phuket

Some people might consider the term 'affordable luxury' an oxymoron. But those unlucky people must never have experienced life at Twinpalms Phuket. The Thai island's latest contemporary resort brings new meaning to luxury hospitality, sans the stratospheric price tag.

Just 25 minutes away from Phuket airport, this stylish boutique hotel brings together the exclusiveness of a secluded getaway with all the modern conveniences that will keep you rooted to your every day world. Couple all that with a level of service that is both friendly and impeccably professional, and you get a dream resort worthy of all your precious vacation days.

76 spacious guest rooms are set around a beautiful pool, each decked out in sleek minimalist lines. Swish, contemporary furnishings adorn each room, from oversized beds with mattresses that are too comfortable for words, to rain and hand showers that elevate every bathtime to an exquisite experience. Whether you're basking in your bathtub or lazing on your private balcony, the views of the resort's splendidly landscaped gardens will be absolutely spectacular.

...a dream resort worthy of all your precious vacation days.

THIS PAGE (FROM TOP): *A lush tropical water garden meanders serenely around the whole Twinpalms Phuket resort; East meets West with clean minimalism and a Thai twist.*

OPPOSITE (FROM TOP): *Comfort and chic make a happy pairing; sinking into crisp white linen must be one of life's most underrated pleasures.*

Touted as a "Garden of Eden for our times", Twinpalms Phuket's tropical water garden binds the entire resort with a calm, emerald pool that flows serenely amongst lush, modern landscaping. East meets West through the use of clean architectural lines and traditional Thai accents, creating a sprawling pool area of 1,600 sq m (17,222 sq ft). As well as being an elegant water feature, it feels like a magical place to unwind. And for those not content with lazing away their days at Twinpalms Phuket, the impressive 50 m (164 ft) pool is a perfect place for diehard athletes to do laps in, blissfully uninterrupted.

The secluded stretch of Surin Beach is less than 200 m (656 ft) away from the resort. If that proves too much of a walk for you, one of the resort's nifty buggies can ferry you to this sandy slice of paradise on what has come to be known as Millionaire's Row (think über-luxury hotels and expensive private residential developments).

But if you prefer to stay within the glorious confines of Twinpalms Phuket—and understandably so—there is also plenty to do. At Palm Spa, a dedicated team of Thai therapists are on hand to nurture your entire well-being, taking a holistic approach of combining Eastern therapies with the latest

Western techniques to help realign your mind, body and spirit. With a strong sense of privacy, luxury and exclusivity, Palm Spa has delicious treatments for both women and men, and prides itself on capturing a seamless fusion between five-star amenities and local ambience. Just one delicate whiff of the comforting essential oil aromas that permeate the spa, and you're already on your way to a more peaceful, centred you. Choose from an extensive menu of treatments that includes Thai massages, firming and relaxing facials and bliss-out Oriental foot rituals.

Entertainment in this haven of serenity can be found in abundance at Twinpalms Phuket's outstanding library that houses its own original art installation of Phuket seascapes. Browse its collection of international magazines, its wide selection of literature from around the world, or pick a movie from its extensive DVD collection to enjoy in the comfort of your room. Complimentary high-speed Internet access also allows guests to keep in touch with what's going on outside of Paradise—that is of course, if you can even remember the busy world outside.

THIS PAGE (FROM TOP): *The immaculate white rooms provide a heavenly escape for those needing time out; clean architectural lines and swish marble terraces bring understated glamour to your pre-dinner drinks.*
OPPOSITE: *The lushness and serenity of Twinpalms Phuket is a giant slice of Paradise.*

Perhaps what is most talked about and admired at Twinpalms Phuket is not its unrivalled service and style, but its restaurant and oyster bar—Oriental Spoon. The sister restaurant to Bangkok's fabulous Kuppa, Oriental Spoon is set in a stunning double-height space, with mobile Thai art and an air-conditioned wine cellar that draws both a crowd of hip locals and discerning hotel guests. Savour authentic Thai and Western cuisine while you watch the buzzing streets outside come alive with people from all walks of life.

Next to Oriental Spoon is Martini Bar, which as its name suggests, serves every flavour of martini that you could possibly desire. Quaff a few chic Cosmopolitans and chase them down with a decadent Chocolate Martini before finishing off with a classic Manhattan "shaken not stirred". And then stroll out into the bright lights of the pretty streets to experience Phuket nightlife at its very best.

When the sun, the martinis and the energetic vibe of the evening have all but worn you out, return to your Twinpalms Phuket villa to sweetly slumber in some of the most comfortable beds this side of the island. Snuggle down and dream of holidays to come—you'll probably already be planning your next stay.

FACTS

ROOMS	76 rooms and suites
FOOD	Oriental Spoon Restaurant and Oyster Bar: Thai and Western • Martini Bar: international • Pool Bar: international
DRINK	Oriental Spoon Restaurant and Oyster Bar • Martini Bar • Pool Bar • Wine Room
FEATURES	Palm spa • lagoon pool • library • high-speed Internet access • business centre • conference room • island shop • Twinpalms beach club
NEARBY	Surin Beach
CONTACT	106/46 Moo 3, Surin Beach Road, Cherng Talay, Phuket 83110 • telephone: +66.76 316 500 • facsimile: +66.76 316 599 • email: book@twinpalms-phuket.com • website: www.twinpalms-phuket.com

Rayavadee

Graciousness and warmth are at the heart of Rayavadee, Krabi's most luxurious resort and a member of The Leading Hotels of the World. From the moment you step off the resort's private boat onto the pristine shores of Nam Mao Beach, the resort's staff will welcome you with the best of Thai hospitality and five-star service combined.

This dreamy hideaway is a glorious gem engraved on a small peninsula and flanked by three beaches. Hugging the property is Cape Phra Nang, where the crystal-clear waters of the Andaman Sea encircle soaring limestone cliffs and

neighbouring islands. Adjacent to the resort is the verdant Marine National Park, rife with wild monkeys and exotic birdlife.

Spread over 11 hectares (26 acres) of coconut grove, Rayavadee's award-winning architecture and tropical landscaping were designed after a Southern Thai village. It boasts six impressive villas and 98 luxurious two-storey pavilions built as hexagonal-shaped cottages with high-domed roofing. These pavilions are categorised into different groups and offer different features—garden, deluxe, spa and hydro pool. Spa pavilions come with a

THIS PAGE: Three stunning beaches, including Cape Phra Nang, surround Rayavadee.

OPPOSITE (FROM LEFT) Rich earthy hues and woods set the tone in the Master Suite of the Raitalay Villa, and in the pavilions; a magical glow of the pavilions at sundown within the lush landscape.

private garden and a jacuzzi, while Hydro Pool pavilions are built in a walled garden with a fresh water hydro pool, sundeck and barbecue terrace for outdoor dining.

Enter any of its rooms and the sweet perfume of jasmine drifts through the air. All its king-sized beds are adorned with earth-toned fabrics and natural materials, while bathtubs are thoughtfully built for two. Guests are never left hungry thanks to a continuous supply of mineral water, coffee, tea, handcrafted chocolates and homemade chocolate chip cookies throughout their stay. Still, one cannot live on chocolate alone. The epicurean pleasures at Rayavadee are certainly in a stratosphere of their own. The Raitalay Terrace, located beside the capacious swimming pool and Railay Beach, is well known for its spectacular sunsets. Enjoy a cocktail while you revel in its beauty. Or perhaps enjoy a barbecue by soaring limestone cliffs and sugary sands at The Grotto, on the other side of the island. For more hearty fare, Raya Dining serves an array of Thai and international dishes in an elegant yet casual setting. Otherwise, take a leisurely stroll to the romantic Krua Phranang Restaurant and Bar to savour the intricate flavours of southern Thailand.

With famous neighbours such as the gorgeous Koh Phi Phi just a hop away, simply take the resort speedboat and head out. But if you prefer your vacations relaxed, head to Rayavadee's exquisite spa which will remind you just how far away from the frenzied world you've come.

FACTS		
	ROOMS	98 pavilions • 6 villas
	FOOD	The Grotto: barbecues upon request • Raya Dining: Thai and Western • Krua Phranang: Traditional Thai and seafood • Raitalay Terrace: international light meals
	DRINK	Raya Lounge
	FEATURES	spa • non-motorised sea sports • meeting facilities • boutique • library • pool • tennis courts • squash court • fitness centre
	NEARBY	Phi Phi island • Bamboo island • Poda island
	CONTACT	214 Moo 2, Tambol Ao-Nang, Amphur Muang, Krabi 81000 • telephone: +66.75.620 740-3 • facsimile: +66.75.620 630 • email: reservation@rayavadee.com • website: www.rayavadee.com

PHOTOGRAPHS COURTESY OF RAYAVADEE.

Sheraton Krabi Beach Resort

The backdrop for the Sheraton Krabi Beach Resort is as perfect as a postcard picture. All around it, spectacular towering cliff formations flank lush forests bursting at the seams with flora and fauna. Gaze further ahead and these give way to waters teeming with marine life and coral reefs.

As the province's only international deluxe resort on the 500 m (1,640 ft) stretch of Klong Muong Beach, the Sheraton Krabi could easily have been a concrete mammoth without consideration for its environment. Thankfully, the 16-hectare (40-acre) property has been delicately and eco-consciously set in one of Asia's most fascinating ecosystems—the mangrove, reflecting the extreme and ancient beauty that surrounds Krabi.

Contemporary Thai architecture featuring pavilions, ponds, motifs, vast spaces and high ceilings is juxtaposed with texture and colour. All rooms command views of either

THIS PAGE (FROM TOP): Spoil yourself at the Mandara Spa; or relax by the beautifully landscaped pool with its radiant bougainvillea; warm earth tones and rich woods in the Executive Suite.

OPPOSITE: The resort's spacious, open-concept lobby.

Klong Muong Beach or the resort's impeccable, landscaped gardens. Each is equipped with all the modern amenities a 21st-century guest would expect: space, style, 24-hour room service and Internet connection.

This is a resort where you can do everything or absolutely nothing at all. Spend all afternoon out on the deck overlooking the infinity-edge pool or ask for a kayak and head up towards Krabi's stunning coastline. Take an elephant trek, learn to dive, try a yoga class, or just sit back with a cool cocktail at any of the resort's five bars and restaurants. All offer al fresco eating options, allowing guests to take advantage of the gorgeous weather and stunning views of the Andaman's pristine waters. Martinis, in particular, is reputed to serve up the best martini in south Thailand—it's worth a visit for that alone. Alternatively, hire a bike at sunset and take a ride along the picturesque seashore.

The resort's unrivalled luxury is highlighted by the peaceful Mandara Spa. Blending traditional beauty elixirs with Eastern rejuvenation secrets, the spa offers a long list of life's little luxuries—massages, scrubs, wraps, steams, facials and exotic soaks. You can choose to have a massage in your room, or better still, poolside, while you absorb the tropical garden setting. Or check into the spa suite and escape for a few hours instead. The suite comes with its own floral bath and steam room. Such bliss.

PHOTOGRAPHS COURTESY OF SHERATON KRABI BEACH RESORT.

FACTS

ROOMS	6 executive suites • 30 zen rooms • 210 rooms
FOOD	Mangosteen's: international • Gecko's: Mediterranean • The Deck: pizza and snacks
DRINK	CocoVida • Martinis
FEATURES	Mandara Spa • tour service • tennis • diving centre
NEARBY	Fossil Shell Beach • elephant trekking • jungle walks • island hopping
CONTACT	155 Moo 2, Nong Thale, Muang Krabi, Krabi 81000 • telephone: +66.75.628 000 • facsimile: +66.75.628 028 • email: sheraton.krabi@sheraton.com • website: www.sheraton.com/krabi

Costa Lanta, Krabi

shut the doors and find yourself in a modish cube-like space, much like a living and breathing art installation. Hide away from the rest of the world, or mingle with other holidaymakers—both are equally easy to do since the resort was designed around the fact that privacy and conviviality are similarly valued.

Once a landscape of tropical pine trees facing the Andaman Sea, Costa Lanta is spread over 2.5 hectares (6.2 acres) of land. While other resorts boast beachfront living mere footsteps away from the sea, Costa Lanta has chosen instead to turn its interests to preserving nature and the environment. Its accommodations are, thus,

It is often a quandary that urbanites face—the desire to escape from the bustle of city life yet not being able to break away from its modern comforts. The creators of Costa Lanta have built a space that bridges this gap seamlessly and stylishly.

Located on the secluded northern end of Koh Lanta's Klong Dao Beach, Costa Lanta is truly unique. Its signature open-box style bungalows seem to intuitively fit your needs. Throw open the front doors and they feel like a stylish tropical garden house;

THIS PAGE (FROM LEFT): The modular design of the beachfront restaurant and bar allows for flexibility in function.

OPPOSITE (FROM LEFT): The stylish superior room, standard room and beachfront restaurant and bar all underline the resort's philosophy—life in the open.

Its signature open-box style bungalows seem to intuitively fit your needs...

inconspicuously hidden away among the tree lines, less than 80 m (262 ft) from the seafront. Minimalism is key to Costa Lanta's design, with angular raw concrete walls softened by sleek wooden panels and crisp, comfortable white linen.

Created by young and upcoming Thai architect Duangrit Bunnag, Costa Lanta boasts a beachfront restaurant and bar and a sleek swimming pool that were built to blend harmoniously with its picturesque

natural landscape. The best time to visit Costa Lanta is between November and the end of April, when the sea is calm and opportunities for adventure abound.

The famous dive sites of Koh Phi Phi, Koh Ha and Hin Deang to Hin Muang are within easy reach of the resort. Enjoy eco-tours like kayaking in the Emerald Caves and through the mangroves of Koh Talabeang. Private tours can also be arranged by renting a traditional long-tail

boat to trip across to Koh Lanta, stopping at its various picturesque beaches along the way. Just chilling out within the resort is an experience unto itself.

Call for a relaxing Thai massage, sip cocktails on the seashore, or munch on delectable Thai and seafood creations at Costa Lanta's beachfront restaurant. Otherwise, stay in bed with a good book and enjoy the swish surrounds of your uniquely designed bungalow.

FACTS

ROOMS	22 bungalows
FOOD	beachfront restaurant
DRINK	beachfront bar
FEATURES	massage at beachfront sala • beachfront pool
NEARBY	elephant trekking • Lanta National Park and lighthouse • sea gypsy village
CONTACT	Bangkok reservation office, 12/24 Sukhumvit Soi 33, Bangkok 10110 • telephone: +66.2.662 3550 • facsimile: +66.2.260 9067 • email: info@costalanta.com • website: www.costalanta.com

PHOTOGRAPHS COURTESY OF COSTA LANTA.

Pimalai Resort + Spa

Just 70 kilometres (43 miles) from Krabi airport is the southern Thai island of Koh Lanta. This undeveloped paradise is lush with verdant greens and azure waters that thrive with colourful marine life. Dive enthusiasts from all over the world flock here to visit the underwater residents, from magnificent manta rays to delicate parrotfish.

Hidden away on this breathtaking island is a five-star resort that overlooks the impossibly blue Andaman Sea. Pimalai, which connotes flower gardens and purity, is the name of this exceptional resort and spa.

A member of Small Luxury Hotels of the World and recipient of the 2004 Thailand Tourism Award for Excellence, it is easy to see why Pimalai is renowned for its peaceful beauty. Terraced lawns and a flight of high-ceiling pavilions shelter Pimalai's dining room, bar and reception areas. Dotted around its fertile landscape are 114 rooms, suites and villas secreted amidst dense foliage with magical glimpses of the sea. All rooms are of generous size, and appointed in understated, contemporary Thai furnishings to emphasise their spaciousness.

THIS PAGE: Watch your own infinity-edge pool melting irresistibly into blue Thai skies.

OPPOSITE (FROM TOP): Pimalai's Pool Villas have their very own spacious sundecks; a lush jungle of casuarinas, cashew and palm plantations surround Pimalai Spa.

Each has a large balcony with sumptuous wooden furniture and a ceiling fan that virtually hypnotises with its cool whirring.

The resort's new one- and two-bedroom Pool Villas boast master bedrooms facing the magnificent Ba Kan Tiang bay; oversized bathrooms with rain showers and large bathtubs; as well as spacious sundecks with private infinity-edge pools. A kitchenette also allows guests to prepare a snack or meal if they so wish.

Pimalai's architecture is thoughtfully enhanced with marble, teak and rattan features for a tropical feel. Step outside these beautifully designed comforts and descend into an almost uninhabited 1-kilometre (½-mile) stretch of beach with dazzling soft white sand.

Swim, snorkel or scuba dive under the golden sun, and catch your private showing of the underwater world's constantly evolving population. Pimalai boasts its own PADI dive centre (from November to April), so whether you're an experienced diver or a beginner, there are classes, programmes and dive tours to help you enjoy one of the best dive spots in the world.

Non-divers will find lots to do here too. Near to the resort are elephant camps which offer spectacular rides on the backs of the animal kingdom's most gentle giants. Or go trekking at the gorgeous Lanta Marine Park where gibbons swing from tree to tree to welcome you, or scuttle along the path beside you. From November to April the

Squid Safari Sunset Cruise provides an excellent experience: learn to catch slippery squids straight from the ocean and then grill them on the barbecue. Otherwise, hop on one of the regular excursions to Koh Lanta's equally awesome neighbouring islands: Koh Gnai for its vast coral reefs or Koh Muk for its stunning Emerald Cave, a 60-m (66-yd) tunnel that runs through a mountain and leads to a tranquil lagoon at the bottom of a sheer vertical shaft.

But if more languorous pursuits are what you're after, head to the Pimalai Spa. Nestled on a lush sloping valley, the Pimalai Spa's sole purpose is to bring its pampered guests back to nature through soothing massages and exquisite spa treatments.

Seven thatch-roofed salas blend seamlessly into the natural beauty of the jungle.

THIS PAGE (CLOCKWISE FROM RIGHT):
Slumber in undisturbed bliss in this bed fit for a king or queen; local chefs create delicious Thai cuisine in the subtly grand Spice 'n Rice restaurant; the Spa jacuzzi is a heavenly hideaway for weary souls.
OPPOSITE: Romantic dining at the beachside Rak Talay.

Here, Japanese fancy carp glide lazily through a bubbling pond that lies beneath sleek wooden walkways. Seven thatch-roofed salas blend seamlessly into the natural beauty of the jungle. Fashioned with stones, native wood, bamboo, iron rope and ceramics, the salas are the perfect setting to lay back and be pampered by the spa's therapists. Choose from a range of massages such as the relaxing Asian Aroma massage or the invigorating Pimalai Sports massage.

But when in Thailand it would seem a waste not to indulge in an authentic Thai massage. And when in Pimalai, the Thai massage is performed in its own special open-air pavilion at the bottom of the valley. Called the Royal Siam massage, Pimalai's technique uses a firm thumb and palm pressure on the body's lines and on pressure points, while manipulating the body into various stretching movements. To enhance this experience, guests can also request the Luk Pra Kohb, a preparation of aromatic Thai herbs used as steaming poultices to deeply massage the body.

Rejuvenated from the Royal Siam experience, head to one of the resort's three excellent restaurants to sample Pimalai's acclaimed cuisine. The Rak Talay Beach Bar and Restaurant serves seafood fresh from the Andaman, prepared especially for you. The Baan Pimalai restaurant, with its sweeping views of the infinity-edge pool, landscaped gardens and bay, has an à la carte menu of Thai and international specialities.

Meanwhile, the Spice 'n Rice restaurant is the place to go for authentic Thai cuisine, cooked by local chefs. After dinner, take a stroll under the inky night sky, studded with countless stars. And when the romance of it all gets the better of you, you can dream up your very own Pimalai wedding.

FACTS	
ROOMS	64 superior rooms • 4 bay front deluxe rooms • 7 pavilion suites • 7 beach villas • 32 pool villas
FOOD	Baan Pimalai: Thai and Western • Spice 'n Rice: Thai • Rak Talay Beach Bar and Restaurant: seafood grill, snacks and Western
DRINK	Pool bar • Lobby bar
FEATURES	spa • pool • library • fitness room • sports equipment • dive centre • trekking • mountain biking • private speedboat rental • private celebrations
NEARBY	Lanta Marine National Park • Koh Muk • Koh Rok • Koh Kradan • elephant camps
CONTACT	99 Moo 5, Ban Kan Tiang Beach, Koh Lanta, Krabi 81150 • telephone: +66.75.607 999 • facsimile: +66.75.607 998 • email: reservation@pimalai.com • website: www.pimalai.com

PHOTOGRAPHS COURTESY OF PIMALAI RESORT + SPA.

SriLanta

Koh Lanta is without doubt one of Thailand's most impressive islands. The scenic fishermen's island in the Krabi province is home to age-old forests, surrounded by the dazzling Andaman Sea. Built on the beach and perched at the edge of the forest, the boutique resort SriLanta blends perfectly into its surroundings to serve as the ideal retreat for city dwellers searching for sun, sea and a dose of nature.

Located approximately 70 km (36 miles) south of Krabi city, SriLanta is accessible from Koh Phi Phi and Krabi by passenger boat. The trip takes a leisurely two hours or so, or an hour if you opt for a speedboat. Yet once you arrive at SriLanta, on this island of sea-gypsies and stunning sunsets, you may never want to leave.

On- and offshore adventure is readily available at SriLanta, as its location is the ideal base for diving and snorkelling excursions to neighbouring islands.

Still, visitors who come here may find little need to venture out. SriLanta boasts 48 chic thatched villas, all minimalist in style and accentuated by natural furnishings. Built on a hillside overlooking the beach, the villas combine luxurious comfort with traditional living.

Inspired by SriLanta's motto, 'the resplendence of life', its designers created a retreat that complements its ecological surroundings: natural textiles, al fresco bathrooms, water walls, and tranquil ponds. The thoughtful placement of the buildings evoke a sense of peace and serenity.

THIS PAGE (FROM TOP): Natural and luxurious—fresh flowers floating in an earthen bath; thatched cottages blend into the leafy surrounds; tea for two in the subtle and sophisticated villa.

OPPOSITE: Bask in the tropical warmth by the pool on a comfortable lounger, sheltered by vibrant umbrellas.

...a retreat that complements its ecological surroundings...

Delightful winding paths link SriLanta's villas to its communal facilities, including the SriSpa. Here, the senses are awakened through healing touch and aromatic oils, all combined with traditional Thai therapies to refresh, rejuvenate and restore.

On SriLanta's pristine slice of beach, laze on a shaded sunbed and sip luscious tropical cocktails from the Beach Bar. Or chill out by the black-tiled pool by the beach and soak up the brilliant tropical sun. Or, if you like, SriLanta can provide activities ranging from yoga and meditation, to sailing, mountain biking and kayaking.

To end a day of lazing under the sky or living it up in Koh Lanta's outdoors, enjoy a sumptuous meal at SriLanta's Surya Chandra restaurant. Built almost entirely from wood and grass, it offers an excellent selection of Thai and international dishes. And if the night is too beautiful for sleep, grab yourself an exotic cocktail (or three) and spend the evening taking in the splendour of SriLanta under a silvery blanket of stars.

PHOTOGRAPHS COURTESY OF SRILANTA.

FACTS	
ROOMS	48 villas
FOOD	Surya Chandra Restaurant: Thai and international • The Chedi Beach Bar: light meals and grilled seafood
DRINK	The Chedi Beach Bar
FEATURES	pool • spa • catamaran sailing • darts • jungle trekking • marine excursions • pétanque (boules) • sea kayaking • windsurfing • yoga • vehicle rentals
NEARBY	Lanta Old Town • Saladan Town • Je Lee Village • Sea Gypsy Village • Tung Yee Pheng Village • Kao Mai Kaeo Cave • Koh Ha Island • Koh Rok Island
CONTACT	111 Moo 6 Klongnin Beach Koh Lanta Yai Krabi 81150 • telephone: +66.75.697 288 • facsimile: +66.75.697 289 • email: srilanta@srilanta.com • website: www.srilanta.com

Zeavola

The charms of rural Thailand have all been brought to the fore at Zeavola, Krabi's latest all-suite boutique hotel on the northern tip of Koh Phi Phi. The name Zeavola derives from the exotic Scaevola Taccado (half flower) tree, better known in Thailand as Rak Talay, meaning 'love the sea'.

Aptly, the resort is set on a prime slice of white-sanded beach, and cost over 400 million baht to build. Its owner, Mr Quanchai Panitpichetvong—himself a well-travelled and experienced hotelier—spared no expense in building his dream and creating the most unique and luxurious boutique resort and spa in Thailand. Indeed, Zeavola is a resort unlike any other. Its 52 deluxe villas are made entirely out of wood, rendering a wonderful Swiss Family Robinson-esque feel. Mr Panitpichetvong's bold streak paid off, as he dared to incorporate designs, shapes and styles unseen in any other resort. The result is a charming property that boasts rural, rustic luxury at its very best.

Understanding that a hotel, no matter how beautiful, is nothing without dedicated staff, Mr Panitpichetvong put together a team of experienced individuals. 170 employees to 52 villas means personalised attention for all who stay at Zeavola. And Mr Panitpichetvong's founding principle, that employees and employer will always work hand in hand, means his staff are well cared for. Training and morale are prioritised so that Zeavola's guests are ensured service which comes straight from the heart.

Just an hour away by speedboat from Phuket or Krabi, Zeavola can boast close proximity to all the magical sights of Koh Phi Phi. A dedicated diving and sports centre within the resort caters to those with an adventurous streak. Diving courses are conducted regularly by PADI-certified instructors, so guests can enjoy exploring the underwater delights of the surrounding waters with expert guidance. From shallow, sheltered bays to wall and drift dives, there is something to please divers of every ability. With weak to moderate currents, visibility in these waters ranges from about 10 to 25 m (33 to 82 ft), making each dive an immensely sublime and pleasurable experience for everyone who ventures below the crystal surface.

Colourful fish, vibrant soft corals and huge sea fans are just some of the amazing natural marine life that thrive in this area. On the sandy bottom of the sea bed, leopard sharks can be found resting among lion fish, groupers and bearded scorpion fish. For those who prefer to stay nearer to the water's surface, snorkelling can be an equally ethereal experience.

To explore further, expeditions to nearby islands can be easily arranged by Zeavola staff. Hop on a traditional long-tail boat to hidden sandy beaches barely touched by the human hand. Windsurfing, kayaking and sailing are also available through the Sports Centre for those not simply content with lazing on the white sands and lapping up the beautiful Thai sun.

THIS PAGE: **The beautifully rustic interiors of Zeavola are effortlessly stylish and comfortable whilst capturing the glamour of a boutique resort.**
OPPOSITE: **Inspired by nature, the peaceful outdoor ambience to the individual bedrooms encourages restful slumber.**

THIS PAGE: *Dining under the stars will leave lasting and wonderful memories of rural Thailand.*

OPPOSITE (FROM LEFT): *Zeavola's private suites provide a luxurious escape; take a moment to enjoy your peaceful surroundings.*

No luxury resort with such rustic charms would be complete without its own dedicated spa. And the Zeavola Spa does not disappoint. With a strong emphasis on nature and inspired by the "charms, scent and joy of rural Thailand", it offers pampering treatments dedicated to invigorating the body and soul while stimulating the senses towards health and contentment. To do this effectively, the spa uses a range of delicious traditional, ethnic and specially imported products and principles which continue to benefit guests long after they leave.

Guests may choose from a tantalising array of exquisite three-hour packages for the ultimate indulgence, or break up the pleasure into daily massages, body wraps, scrubs or beauty treatments to prolong the enjoyment and sense of overall wellbeing.

When your senses are soothed and your body relaxed, satiate your appetite at one of the resort's two excellent restaurants. Baxil serves a menu of authentic Italian cuisine accompanied by an extensive international wine list.

Whether you dine out beneath the stars in a romantic setting or delight your tastebuds in air-conditioned comfort, the standard of food and service you receive is sure to create happy and wonderful memories of your stay on Koh Phi Phi.

Delightfully informal but no less excellent is Zeavola's second restaurant, Tacada. Try its selection of sumptuous Thai cuisine, or opt for international dishes and snacks. Being close to the sea means there is always a bounty of fresh catches ready to be barbecued and served just for you.

At dusk, chill out under the setting sun and watch it disappear below the horizon as you sip on a cool cocktail. As night takes over and brings with it a carpet of silver stars, retire to the quietude of Zeavola's beautifully rustic suites, and slumber to the chorus of nature's sweet sounds.

FACTS		
	ROOMS	52 suites
	FOOD	Baxil: Italian • Tacada: Thai and international
	DRINK	Tacada: beach bar
	FEATURES	tour desk • concierge • boutique • high-speed Internet access • diving and sports centre • spa complex • coiffeur
	NEARBY	Krabi • Phuket
	CONTACT	11 Moo 8 Laem Tong, Koh Phi Phi, Ao Nang, Krabi 81000 • telephone: +66.75.627 000 • facsimile: +66.75.627.025 • email: info@zeavola.com • website: www.zeavola.com

PHOTOGRAPHS COURTESY OF ZEAVOLA.

Amari Trang Beach Resort

Changlang Beach in Trang, Thailand, is famed for the beautiful spiral-shaped shells that abundantly line its white sandy shores. Clear as blue tourmaline, its waters beckon, shaded by whispering casuarina trees.

It is in this tropical paradise that the Amari Trang Beach Resort was built. Just 45 minutes away from Trang airport, the resort is a luxurious sanctuary decked in rich dark woods and earth-toned Thai silks with cream accents. Retreat to one of its 138 seafront rooms and suites, each with its own stylish terrace. From here, sip your sundowner and enjoy spectacular sunsets over the Gulf of Thailand. Adjacent to the resort is the Chao Mai National Park, which stretches over the coastal area and encompasses the many gem-like islands offshore. Explore the small caves that riddle the surrounding limestone cliffs. Or take a leisurely walk along its seemingly endless stretch of beach at dawn or dusk.

Within the resort is a full range of facilities that could see you through hours of blissful relaxation. Chill out by the pool, lounge on sumptuous deck chairs by the pristine beach, work up a sweat at the fitness centre or pamper yourself with indulgent massages and beauty treatments at the Sivara Spa. If you'd like to experience

THIS PAGE (FROM TOP): Relax on the pristine white beaches; the lobby and guestrooms feature warm earth tones and rich silks.

OPPOSITE: Casuarina trees enhance the beautiful landscape of the pool area.

It is in this tropical paradise that the Amari Trang Beach Resort was built.

Thai culture firsthand, the Amari also offers interesting activities like Thai cooking classes conducted by the hotel's chef. Learn to make authentic, tastebud-tingling dishes like the famous Tom Yam Goong and Paad Thai. And if you prefer more gentle options, take a class in the art of batik painting.

A dive centre within the resort is your gateway to the amazing coastal waters of the Andaman around Trang. Large parts of the area have been declared national parks, which means there is plenty of exotic and fascinating sea life to explore. Sharks, manta rays, turtles and even the occasional whale shark have been known to take up residence here; and visibility of up to 20 m (66 ft) is considered the norm.

Nearby, natural wonders abound with waterfalls, caves, mountains, jungles and hot springs. The resort can arrange golf trips to a nearby golf course, island-discovery tours, eco tours, and excursions customised to suit each guest's preferences.

PHOTOGRAPHS COURTESY OF AMARI TRANG BEACH RESORT.

FACTS

ROOMS	6 suites • 46 deluxe rooms • 86 superior rooms
FOOD	Vistas Restaurant: International • Crabs & Co: Thai and seafood • Acqua: Italian
DRINK	Sunset Bar • The Beach House
FEATURES	spa • fitness and activities centres • conference and banquet facilities • dive centre
NEARBY	Krabi • Hin Daeng (Red Rock) and Hin Muang (Purple Rock) dive sites • Khao Chong Wildlife Centre • Khao Pu Khao Ya National Park
CONTACT	199 Moo 5 Had Pak Meng, Changlang Road, Changlang Beach, Tambon Maifad, Amphur Sikao, Trang 92150 • telephone: +66.75.205.888 • facsimile: +66.75.205 899 • email: trangbeach@amari.com • website: www.amari.com

norththailand

China

Vietnam

Myanmar

Laos

Mae Sai

> Phu Chaisai Mountain Resort + Spa

Tachilek

> The Legend Chiang Rai

Chiang Rai

Tham Pla
National Park

Mae Sa

Tha Pai Hot Springs

Mae Hong Son

Samoeng

> Four Seasons Resort Chiang Mai

Doi Suthep

> The Chedi Chiang Mai

Pai

Chiang Mai

> D2 hotel chiang mai

Nan

> Rachamankha Hotel

Doi Inthanon

> Baan Saen Doi Spa

Lampang

> Mandarin Oriental Dhara Dhevi

Chiang Mai

Phae Meuang Phii

Phrae

Bangkok

Cambodia

of misty mountains, hill tribes and temples

North Thailand offers a completely different experience from the cities and beaches of the central and southern regions of the country. The north has long possessed an unsurprisingly magnetic allure for both Thais and travellers, with its cool mountain scenery; picturesque landscape of misty hills; tribe people and magnificent temples. Indeed, this region can be proud of a wonderful and historic civilisation revolving around the riches of the mountains.

Aside from the main northern city of Chiang Mai, with its bounty of shopping and dining, the surrounding areas, Mae Sa and Samoeng, provide plenty to see. With orchid farms, butterfly parks, elephant camps, botanical gardens and antique and handicraft shops, the area exudes a rural charm for visitors of all ages. Chiang Mai is a relaxing place where you can pursue various cultural studies as well. It has become a destination for learning the increasingly popular art of Thai massage. Courses in Buddhist meditation and Thai cooking can also be enjoyed in the area.

For the more intrepid, trekking in the rugged northern hills is one of the biggest attractions of the region, with a chance to see and experience the life of the mysterious hill tribe people residing in these lands. Many trekkers enjoy going on four- or five-day trips, using the cities of Chiang Mai or Chiang Rai as a base. Many trekking routes lead through the hill-tribe villages which are spread along the hills, consisting of simple thatch structures. Treks normally involve daily walks through wooded mountains, with overnight stays in hill-tribe villages.

the fascinating hill tribes

The exotic hill tribes—beautiful, semi-nomadic people who live life according to the centuries-old tribal customs of their ancestors—are one of the principal attractions of northern Thailand. Isolated from modern urban life, they inhabit the mountains, living off the land by growing small crops. They are ethnic minorities with their own languages, customs, dress, and religious beliefs. Most of the hill tribes migrated to this

THIS PAGE: Akha hill-tribe people are among the many tribes that make their home in Thailand's northern hills.
OPPOSITE: The mist shrouded valley of Mae Hong Son is best viewed from a hillside temple in the morning.

region from Tibet, Myanmar, China and Laos over the past 200 years. They are thought of as 'fourth world people' because they pledge allegiance to no country in particular. These people have a certain ethnic appearance, different from the Thai people of the central and southern regions of the country. Some of the tribal people look more Tibetan in their origins than Thai.

There are over 10 separate and officially recorded hill tribes in Thailand today. The main tribes you can see in the region are the Shan, Lisu, Lahu, Akha, Karen, Kayah, Hmong and Mien. One of the largest groups is the Shan, which is not officially considered 'hill tribe' as its people are thought to be the original inhabitants of the region. The Shan also spread across Myanmar. They own permanent land and speak their own Thai Yai tongue.

Colourful garments distinguish the various tribes from one another. Some tribes wear headdresses fashioned from beads and feathers, lovingly adorned with dangling silver ornaments. Indeed, the hill tribes are well known for their gorgeous handcrafted textiles and exquisitely embroidered materials in brilliant colours and patterns. The textiles they use are usually made from black, white and indigo cotton, which is decorated with striking geometric embroidery.

Tribal textiles are also popular shopping items in Chiang Mai, used for cushions, bedspreads, table linen and clothing. Fabrics produced by the Thai Lu tribe from the Nan province are the most prized in northern Thailand. These fabrics typically feature red and black floral, geometric and animal designs on white cotton. A favourite is the 'flowing water' style, creating patterns that represent streams, rivers and waterfalls.

Perhaps the best known and most fascinating presence within the hill tribes is the long-necked Padaung women, thus described because they don thick brass coils around their necks and legs, resulting in their elongated, giraffe-like aspect. The brass coils can weigh from five to 22 kg (49 lb) and reach up to 30 cm (11 in) in height.

There are a number of Padaung villages frequented as tourist attractions. There, the women obtain an income from visitors who pay a fee to enter the village and take photographs of them. Despite the human rights controversy surrounding this type of tourism, it is the sole way of earning money for many of the tribes in Thailand. For those in exile from their native lands in Myanmar, their life here is a better alternative to the exploitation and hardship they would otherwise face in their country of origin.

'land of a million rice fields'

In Thailand, the word 'Lanna' refers both to the country's northern culture, and also a distinctive style with strong Burmese influences. The Lanna heritage, which is permeated with mystique and wonder, encompasses its very own geography, people, history, architecture, food, and way of life.

Northern Thailand was the location of the country's first true kingdoms. And it is the area's relative isolation from the cultural influences of the central and southern regions that has kept Lanna culture unique over the centuries. The first northern kingdoms began life as small chiefdoms and city-states, but were eventually merged into a much larger kingdom known as Lanna in the 14th century. Lanna also signifies 'Land of a Million Rice Fields', and the kingdom covered what are now eight provinces. Lanna society today thus fittingly thrives on rice cultivation and the yield of the surrounding forestlands.

lanna: a unique architectural style

Lanna architecture is easily recognisable, and differs markedly from the classic style of the central plains. Lanna temples are topped with multi-tiered roofs—bigger and more sloping than classic Thai ones—and the ornamentation makes great use of coloured-glass mosaic work. Northern temples were specifically placed in each city centre or on the highest part of a settlement, with a wall encircling the temple compound. Some of the most sublime instances of classic Lanna temple style can still be found around the cities of Chiang Mai and Lampang.

THIS PAGE: Terraced rice paddies glow emerald green in the fertile north.

OPPOSITE (FROM TOP): Simple hill-tribe villages along the popular trekking routes; exquisite embroidery and metal coins are trademarks of hill-tribe textiles, as seen on this White Hmong costume; some tribal women possess incredible elongated necks, due to an ancient custom where brass rings are worn on their necks and legs.

Old Lanna temple murals depict religious themes from the life of Buddha, and scenes from everyday life in earlier times. These illustrations showcase Lanna customs, agricultural and religious practices, and textiles. In temple murals in the Chiang Mai and Nan areas, you can see the hairstyles, headdresses and clothes that people once wore and considered fashionable. These artworks even depict patterns on clothes, revealing that courtiers back then wore cottons from Gujarat in western India.

symbols of wealth and fertility

Northern Thai houses can claim a style all their own too. While houses in the central plains are known by their steep pointing gables, a northern structure is more often mounted with a carved V-shaped ornamentation—kalae—on the apex of the roof gable. Strangely, the origins of the kalae carving remain unknown. In some houses, the kalae are carved to look like the wings of a bird in flight. However, it is also said that

the kalae are meant to resemble buffalo horns. Kalae are usually found only on upper-class houses, and the design may have originated from the ancient custom of placing buffalo horns on the roof of a home to indicate that the owners were wealthy. The degree of complexity of the carvings corresponded to the wealth of the family.

Another key characteristic of the northern house is the carved lintel, usually with floral, geometric or cloud motifs, above the owner's bedroom door. This lintel is called ham yon, meaning 'magic testicles' in ancient northern language. The lintel represents the fertility of the owners and designates the bedroom as the core of the house. Before the lintel is carved, the homeowner has to perform a ceremony inviting magical powers to enter the lintel, ensuring the couple's fertility.

kantoke dinners

The cuisine in Thailand's north is flavoured with its own individuality. Northern food is generally consumed using hands instead of utensils like forks and spoons. The staple food of Northern Thais is sticky rice, which is firm and glutinous, instead of the boiled, soft white rice of the central plains. Savouring these chewy viands means breaking a bite-sized chunk from a serving basket, rolling it into a ball, and dipping it in chilli pastes. Northern curries are less rich than their central and southern counterparts.

Pork dishes are plentiful in northern fare. There are many interesting sausages such as the fermented sour pork sausage called name, and sai oua, the cooked pork sausage with a spicy, smoky taste. Crispy pork skin ordinarily appears in every meal, and is dipped in many chilli pastes for added crunch, texture and tang. Among the many chilli pastes in Thai cuisine, there is a distinctive northern version of dipping sauce called nam prik ong, used to flavour boiled vegetables and crispy pork skin.

Like most of northern Thai culture, there is a noticeable Burmese influence in some of the dishes. The most famous noodle dish is khao soi, made of egg noodles covered in a kind of curry gravy with chicken, pork or beef. Topping it off is a fresh sprinkling of diced shallots, pickled cabbage, bean sprouts, shredded raw cabbage, a squeeze of lime for zest, and a dollop of chilli paste for added fire. Making mouth-watering khao soi is quite an art. Strangely, it can be rather difficult to find truly good khao soi restaurants, even in Chiang Mai where the dish originated.

The kantoke dinner is the signature northern meal, utterly captivating with the novel manner in which it is prepared and enjoyed. The meal is served on a low, round woven bamboo table called a kantoke, and is eaten while sitting on the floor on reed mats and cushions—hence the term 'kantoke dinner'. However, the kantoke is actually more of a large tray with a foot base, like a miniature table for one person. Kantoke tables come in many styles, from the most humble basketware to elegant wooden pieces. These popular tray tables are both exotic and functional. They are often prized as chic sofa trays and serving trays on daybeds for contemporary Thai décor.

THIS PAGE: The northern kantoke dinner consists of an enticing array of many small dishes presented on an individual dining tray.

OPPOSITE (FROM TOP): A mural at Wat Phumin in Nan shows beautifully detailed depictions of historical hair styles and textile patterns; a classic northern house is distinguished by the V-shaped kalae carving on its roof.

Each kantoke is meant for an individual diner and bears small bowls of various dishes. The usual assortment consists of one dry curry, one chilli paste, one pickled sausage dish, a vegetable one, and some crispy pork skin to dip into the chilli paste. Sticky rice is provided in a small basket container, and as the repast is eaten with the hands, a finger bowl is available for rinsing.

The much-loved northern fruit, the longan, is grown in many people's gardens as well as being cultivated in orchards. Strawberries were once rare and expensive imported foreign fruits, but are now cultivated in the north too. You can buy succulent fresh berries at street vendors around Chiang Mai, and also in Bangkok supermarkets.

a coveted rustic retreat

Once a sleepy town, Chiang Mai is now the second city of Thailand and the trading centre for the north, handling business between its neighbours Myanmar and Laos. While undergoing a current building boom, the city guards its rural charm, making it one of the most pleasant places to live. For many Thai denizens of Bangkok, securing a second home in Chiang Mai is a dream. It is a retreat from the heat of the plains, with its cool climate, natural environment, rustic and laidback atmosphere, and—most importantly for food-loving Thais—northern cuisine. While foreign visitors flock to the southern beaches and islands during the cool months of November to January, urban Thais take refuge in the north. This is their annual chance to experience cooler days with chilly mornings and evenings, and wear a sweater for a change!

Not that long ago, accommodation in Chiang Mai was mostly middle-market resorts and backpacker guesthouses. It is now the target for top-of-the-line hotels. The Four Seasons Chiang Mai used to be the only luxury resort in the area, but it is now facing competition from the lavish magnificence of the Mandarin Oriental Dhara Dhevi and the upcoming Chedi. Smaller boutique hotels and a flourishing of day spas are changing the face of Chiang Mai's hospitality scene too. The city is on the wave of the newest style trends, but happily still retains its idyllic country-town ambience.

a cultural centre of art and religion

The great King Mengrai, who hailed from Chiang Rai on the Laos-Burma border, founded the city of Chiang Mai (also spelt 'Chiangmai') in 1296, and eventually extended his kingdom into parts of Burma (now Myanmar) and Laos. In the 14th and 15th centuries, Chiang Mai was consolidated into the Lanna Kingdom, which stretched south as far as Kamphaeng Phet and north as far as Luang Prabang in Laos. During this period, Chiang Mai blossomed as a religious and cultural centre. In 1775, the city came under the rule of the Bangkok monarch, King Taksin, who appointed Chao Kavila from Lampang as the viceroy of northern Thailand. Under Kavila, Chiang Mai developed into a prime regional trade hub, conducting brisk trade with Burma. Chiang Mai also evolved into a key location for handicrafts such as ceramics, weaving, silverwork and woodcarving, and it remains so to this day.

Due to its geographical location, the north was isolated from the other Thai kingdoms in the central and southern regions for many centuries, and was able to form an entirely unique cultural identity. It was not until 1921 that the construction of a railway made the region more accessible.

a landscape of temples

Old temples are an integral part of Chiang Mai's appeal, and no visit to the city is complete without a trip to Doi Suthep, the small mountain just outside Chiang Mai, where the famed temple of Wat Phra That Doi Suthep stands. Established in 1383, this is one of the most sacred temples in Northern Thailand, and is named after the hermit Sudeva, who lived on the mountain for many years.

THIS PAGE: The imposing Dhara Dhevi Spa at the Mandarin Oriental Dhara Dhevi hotel in Chiang Mai is modelled on a Burmese palace in Mandalay.

OPPOSITE (FROM TOP): Contemporary chic is the design buzz at The Chedi hotel in Chiang Mai; the blossom-strewn lawn at the Mandarin Oriental Dhara Dhevi is a tranquil place to meditate.

THIS PAGE (FROM TOP): *Traditional Lanna clothing at a wedding; chedis containing the ashes of the royal family of Chiang Mai at Wat Suan Dok.*

OPPOSITE (FROM TOP): *A procession of monks at Wat Phra Singh; the chapel at Wat Thon Kwain and its beautiful ceiling.*

The temple has become an iconic image of Chiang Mai, thanks to the Naga staircase with its much-photographed 300 steps. The stunning chedi of shining copper—topped by a shimmering five-tiered golden umbrella—is one of the holiest chedis in Thailand, and all Thais come here seeking blessings, and praying for wishes to be granted.

Chiang Mai simply abounds in temples. A number are in partial ruins—testimony to their historic significance. Many others are classic examples of northern temples and dotted around the city. The oldest is Wat Chiang Man, situated in the old city. Founded by King Mengrai in 1296, the temple exemplifies the typical Lanna style of temple architecture. It also houses two important Buddha images: the Phra Sil, which is a marble bas relief Buddha said to have come from Sri Lanka; and the renowned Phra Satan Man, a small, exquisite seated crystal Buddha image that travelled much between Thailand and Laos before settling into its current home.

Another fabulous example of a classic Lanna temple is Wat Phra Singh, erected in the 14th century. It houses a well-known image called the Phra Singh Buddha, thought to have originated from Sri Lanka. This image is identical to two other images in Nakhon Si Thammarat and Bangkok. Of the three Buddha images, no one can tell the real one apart from the replicas.

Wat Chedi Luang is a temple complex sheltering an enormous Lanna-style chedi from the 15th century. It is a lovely area with beautiful ancient trees. In 1475, it was home to the famous Emerald Buddha, which now resides in Bangkok's Grand Palace. A jade replica of the image, called Phra Kaew Yok Chiang Mai or the 'Holy Jade Image of Chiang Mai', remains in Wat Chedi Luang. This replica was donated by the current Thai monarch—Bhumibhol Adulyadej—in 1995 for the city's 700th-anniversary celebrations and the chedi's 600th anniversary. Next door to Wat Chedi Luang is the magnificent old Wat Phan Tao, made of teak, supported by 28 massive teak pillars and decorated with coloured mirror mosaic bargeboards. Inside, you can view some old Lanna-style wooden Buddha images and manuscript cabinets, which hold ancient religious manuscripts on palm leaf.

a fine tradition of handicrafts

Through the centuries, Chiang Mai has been renowned for handicrafts. Thanks to an abundance of natural resources like wood, metal and clay, veritable works of art such as woodcarving, lacquer-ware, silver work, ceramics and ivory work flourished here. Around Chiang Mai, artisan communities used to exist as separate villages specialising in particular crafts. Today, the handicraft tradition continues, with valuable skills handed down from generation to generation.

   One of the unique handicrafts of the north is lacquerware, crafted into trays, cups, vases, plates, boxes and other household items. Popular northern-style furnishing objects made from lacquer-ware are octagonal folding tables with engravings. Lacquerware is created by applying lacquer from the Melanorrhea usitata tree over a woven frame to form objects with a hard, glossy sheen. The woven frame is usually made of bamboo. In very high quality items, small cups and bowls consist of horsetail hairs, which give

the item a delicate flexibility. You can identify a top-grade bowl by squeezing the rim until the edges meet—high-quality ones will bounce back into their original shape.

The woven item is then coated with lacquer and left to dry for a few days, after which it is sanded with rice husk ash. Then another coat of lacquer is applied. More exquisite items can have up to seven coats of lacquer. The lacquerware is engraved and painted, then polished to leave the paint in the engraved lines. Multicoloured items are produced using repeated applications of paint. A five-coloured piece can take up to six months to finish. The precision of the engraving is yet another sign of its value.

shopping heaven

The Chiang Mai night bazaar is one of the most popular shopping venues in Thailand, as well as a major tourist attraction. The bazaar extends along the main stretch of Chang Khlan Road to Tha Phae and Si Donchai Roads. It is open every day, come rain or shine. By day, it appears as an ordinary thoroughfare, but when night falls, it assumes another personality altogether. The streets are lined with vendors selling almost anything you can imagine—handicrafts, clothes, fake designer

goods, bags, shoes, CDs, ceramics and souvenirs. With luck, you may even spot some funky clothes and accessories from India and Nepal. And you will see hill-tribe vendors in their tribal costumes plying tribal jewellery, beads and textiles. Although prices at the market are astoundingly affordable, part of the fun is in bargaining.

Chiang Mai is also the right place to purchase outstanding furniture and home décor items. Nimanheman Road, the city's trendiest street, is paved with the most stylish contemporary home décor shops like Gong Dee and Ayodhya. Many antique shops are located along Tha Phae Road, offering numerous Burmese artefacts as well as antique Burmese furniture in the British colonial style. Chiang Mai is where you can get your hands on reproductions of Thai and Burmese antique furniture and custom-made furniture of old salvaged teak.

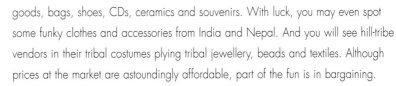

a fun-loving city

As a tourist haven, university town and regional trade hub, the city of Chiang Mai leads an energetic and youthful nightlife, boasting many pubs and restaurants packed with fun-loving local Thai people as well as visitors. Along the banks of the Ping river, a stretch of restaurant pubs like the Riverside, River View, and The Gallery offer good food and a riverside ambience. Some have live music, including rock and pop favourites performed by local bands.

'gateway to the golden triangle'

Chiang Rai is Thailand's northern-most province and borders three countries—Thailand, Myanmar and Laos—earning its nickname: 'gateway to the Golden Triangle'. Chiang Rai is mountainous country, and its former mystique was derived from its main crop of opium poppies, though crop substitution and other royal development projects have replaced poppies with strawberries, tea, coffee, corn, and fruit crops.

The main city is Chiang Rai, and was founded by King Mengrai in 1262 as part of the Lanna kingdom. Chiang Rai is not as big or bustling as Chiang Mai, and most people use it as a base for trekking around the area. Trekking routes take you through scenic hills and through the villages of the Lahu, Mien, Akha and Lisu tribes. There are shopping places for northern handicrafts, silver and antiques. A night market also offers such goods, although it is smaller than the famous one in Chiang Mai.

A popular activity in Chiang Rai involves hiring a long-tail boat and taking a trip on the Kok river. An

THIS PAGE: *Chic riverside dining is a must at one of the many charming eateries lining the Ping river in Chiang Mai.*

OPPOSITE (FROM TOP): *The north is known for producing lovely Thai ceramics, such as this celadonware from Mengrai kilns in Chiang Mai; lacquerware is a popular item to purchase in the north; Chiang Mai is a wonderful place for sourcing antiques and contemporary furniture.*

afternoon spent floating down the river past exquisite scenery is very enjoyable. Visit the Lahu and Karen hill tribe villages, and take a elephant ride along the way.

Around the area are a number of rustic guesthouses, with many of these organising hikes into the mountains or rafting trips down the river. Scores of travellers make boat trips as part of their memorable journey to Chiang Rai, with the pretty country town of Tha Ton as their starting point.

a land of sunflowers

Mae Hong Son is in Thailand's most northeastern province and sits along the Myanmar border. So much of its allure lies in its Burmese cultural influences, present in temples and building styles. This lovely rural area is home to many Burmese immigrants and hill tribes, mostly the Karen and Shan, along with the Lisu, Hmong and Lahu. The province often conjures up in people's minds an image of its enchanting mist and fog blanketing its valley and hill, picturesque against the thickly forested mountains.

The town of Mae Hong Son is a small provincial capital nestled in a valley which borders Myanmar. Mae Hong Son is quaint and quiet, with a charming lake called Jong Kham Lake—a popular destination on the tourist trail which is marked by a good number of guesthouses and hotels. The population is predominantly Shan so there are several ornate Burmese-style temples.

West of the town, a Shan-style temple perches on the peak of the hill called Doi Kong Mu. A climb in the early hours of the day affords an ethereal vision of the sea of fog that collects over the valley every morning.

Trekking around Mae Hong Son is common, with several guesthouses found along the trekking routes through surrounding valleys, passing Shan and Lahu villages. Discover some of the most beautiful scenery in Mae Hong Son around the area of a Shan village called Mae La-Na, with forests, mountains, streams and limestone caves.

Mae Hong Son is also celebrated among Thai people as the place of blooming sunflower fields and as an escape from the tropical heat of Bangkok. In October and

November, the surrounding hills burst into a spectacular carpet of bright yellow flowers. Admirers come from all over Thailand to revel in the blossoms and the cooler air. The weather turns quite chilly here during the cool season.

Located 17 kilometres (11 miles) northeast of the town is Tham Pla National Park. It is a small attraction and its main draw is the Tham Pla or 'Fish Cave', an unusual structure with a large pond running through it. The pond provides the habitat for hundreds of enormously fat toro brook carp. These fish are deemed sacred by the locals who do not catch or eat them. People feed them fruits and vegetables because they are believed to be vegetarian fish. You can buy fish food from the vendor at the park entrance and watch as the fish throng up to you to feed. The size and number of these creatures make an exciting sight to behold.

THIS PAGE: Every October and November the hills around Mae Hong Son are carpeted with bright yellow sunflowers as far as the eye can see.

OPPOSITE (FROM TOP): The quiet northern charm of Mae Hong Son appeals to nature lovers; Lisu tribes-people celebrate the New Year in the Chiang Rai province.

travelling on the border

Mae Sai's claim to fame is its location as Thailand's northernmost point, where many travellers set out to explore the Golden Triangle area, Doi Tung and Mae Salong. As Mae Sai is one of the few official land crossings open between Thailand and Myanmar, the key attraction here is the Burmese border town of Tachilek. The highlight of the Burmese town is the local market where visitors can buy Burmese lacquerware, gems, jade and other goods from Myanmar and Laos. From Mae Sai, nature lovers can also explore the nearby caves of Tham Luang, blessed with breathtaking crystal formations, and Tham Pum and Tham Pla, caves containing freshwater caverns.

a stronghold of classic northern style

The city of Lampang in the Lampang province is another citadel of northern charm. Thais call it the 'Horse Cart Town' because horse carts still remain as a form of public transport, although they are used mainly by tourists these days. Steeped in history, Lampang is the site of one of Thailand's ancient city-states.

In the 7th century, Lampang formed part of the Hariphunchai kingdom and was said to have been founded by the son of Hariphunchai's queen. In the 19th century, Lampang became an important international teak-trading centre, proof of which is still visible in the town's architecture. Wealthy teak merchants who prospered in the city helped sponsor the construction of many beautiful temples, employing Burmese and Shan artists. These temples have made the city famous for its examples of architecture that are distinctly northern in character.

Lampang is also renowned for the magnificent temple Wat Phra That Lampang Luang, located 18 km (11 miles) southwest of the city. Encircled by ancient Banyan trees that impart a dreamy air to the area, this temple is regarded as the most beautiful in northern Thailand, and is a perfect example of Lanna-style temple architecture. The temple complex's principal feature is the Wihan Luang, with a triple-tiered wooden roof supported by teak pillars. Built in 1476, it is known as the oldest existing wooden

building in Thailand. The inner walls of the building show wonderful 19th-century murals with scenes from the life of Buddha.

Another beautiful temple in Lampang is Wat Phra Kaew Don Tao. It has historical significance because, like Wat Chedi Luang, it was once home to the Emerald Buddha. Lanna religious artefacts are on display at the temple's Lanna Museum. Wat Si Rong Meuang's distinctive multi-tiered roofs, with intricate wooden carving around the gables, is an example of Shan-style temple architecture, influenced by the Shan Burmese people who were wood traders in this area. Another beautiful temple complex is Wat Chedi Sao, owing its name to the 20 white Shan-style chedis in the compound. The temple is the abode of a solid gold, seated Buddha image, dating from the 15th century. Showcased in a glass pavilion on top of a pond, the figure was supposedly found by a farmer in nearby ruins.

Ancient homes also feature strongly in Lampang's landscape. The town's wealthy teak merchants raised lovely teak shop houses and ornate Burmese-style teak mansions covered with remarkable woodcarvings. One of the most well-known examples of a traditional northern Thai house is Baan Sao Nak, or 'House of Many Pillars'. Built in 1896 by a flourishing teak merchant, the enormous structure rests on the top of 116 tall teak pillars, and is completely furnished with Burmese and Thai antiques. Once the private property of the original owners' granddaughter, the house is now a museum. The former owners' collection of antique silverwork, lacquerware, bronzeware and other northern handicrafts are on display.

Aside from excellent architecture, Lampang is known as an elephant-training centre. The Thai Elephant Conservation Centre is located 37 km (23 miles) northwest of the town and is devoted to the conservation, training, care and treatment of elephants, as well as the promotion of eco tourism. The centre is something of a tourist attraction as well, offering an elephant show, exhibits on the history and culture of elephants, and elephant rides in the surrounding forest. Every morning, you can see the elephants bathing in the river—and the animals love being fed by visitors.

THIS PAGE (FROM LEFT): Elephants hauling lumber in the north; elephant trekking is both an exciting and traditional way to explore the jungle.

OPPOSITE (FROM TOP): A farmer crosses a wooden bridge with his wares for the market; take a piece of your adventure home with you by learning how to create classic Thai cuisine.

a slice of bohemian life

Once a sleepy country town with the nearby hot springs as its main attraction, Pai has in recent years developed an artistic community. Many urban creative types have come to settle in Pai, bestowing an attractive bohemian nature on the town. Pai has therefore become a hangout for artists and painters, and the shops reflect this arty feel—with small galleries, art studios and vegetarian cafes. There are a couple of bars throbbing with the rhythms of live blues, jazz and rock performed by musicians who have moved here from Bangkok and Chiang Mai.

In Pai, you can take classes in Thai cooking, batik making, art and Thai massage. It is a relaxing place for visitors to unwind. The local beauty of the rice terraces, hills, waterfalls and hill tribe villages is appreciated by all who are lucky enough to see it.

A number of tasteful bungalow resorts have sprung up, with nature and ecology as their key decorative notes. Most of the bungalows here are of the bamboo and thatch cottage variety. Nearer to the hot spring area, there are a couple of resorts with hot natural mineral water piped into the showers.

The whole town is easy to walk around on foot, or explore by motorbike. Nearby are the Thai Poi Hot Springs, a local park with several bathing areas where visitors can indulge themselves in the natural springs. Pai can also be a great base for trekking, rafting and elephant riding. Try a two-day white-water rafting expedition from Pai to Mae Hong Son, and see a waterfall, fossil reef and hot springs along the way. The main rafting season is during and after the rainy season, from July to December.

doi suthep national park

Doi Suthep is a mountain park located 16 km (10 miles) outside Chiang Mai. It is the park area surrounding the famous Wat Phra That Doi Suthep, one of the north's most sacred temples. The mountain park is marked by extensive hiking trails, some of which pass among hill tribe villages. This mountain is ideal for bird watching and is home to over 300 species of birds. The lush ferns and flowers are a boon for nature lovers.

the delight of nature lovers

This mountain park surrounds Doi Inthanon, Thailand's highest peak, which has always been much admired for its misty views. Within the park are picnic areas, food vendors and three huge waterfalls. The 47 km (29 miles) road to the summit is peppered with photographic opportunities, passing scenic rice fields, picturesque valleys and a good number of small Hmong and Karen tribal villages.

Doi Inthanon is one of the favourite destinations in the whole of Southeast Asia for bird watching. Indeed, this mountain is home to more species of birds than any other region in Thailand. Naturalists come to enjoy the profusion of orchids, lichens, mosses, and an amazing 400 species of birds. Moreover, Doi Inthanon is lucky to one of the remaining habitats of the Asiatic black bear, the Assamese macaque and other rare species of monkeys and gibbons. It is also home to the Indian civet, barking deer and the incredible flying squirrel. These creatures are amongst more than 75 mammal species which reside in the lush habitat of Doi Inthanon.

bizarre formations of the landscape

The unspoilt and rugged Nan province of Thailand possesses a few national parks— well worth visiting for stunning scenery and interesting quirks of nature. One of these parks is the Tham Pha Tup Forest Reserve, a limestone cave complex which lies about 10 km (6 miles) north of Nan, housing many accessible stalactites and stalagmites. Another unique natural landscape feature in the north is Sao Din, or 'Earth Pillars'. The place earned its name because of the strange columns of earth which stick out from a barren valley, about 60 km (37 miles) south of Nan.

A similarly bizarre landscape formation can be found in the Phrae province. Named Phae Meuang Phii, or 'Phae ghost town', geology here has oddly conspired to form pillars of rock and soil that look eerie and ghostly. In spite of its spooky feel and somewhat uncanny character, Phae Meuang Phii is a provincial park and conveniently serviced with tables and food vendors at the entrance.

THIS PAGE (FROM TOP): The golden chedi at Wat Phra That Doi Suthep is a glittering sight; butterfly and orchid farms are popular tourist attractions around Chiang Mai.

OPPOSITE: The route to Pai meanders through lush and tranquil hills such as these.

...the summit is peppered with photographic opportunities...

The Legend Chiang Rai

Set romantically on the Mae Kok river, The Legend Chiang Rai Boutique River Resort and Spa is an oasis of luxury in an area that is rustically undeveloped. Boasting contemporary Lanna-style buildings amongst beautifully landscaped surroundings, the resort sits close to the Golden Triangle, at the confluence of Burma, Laos and China.

Warm woods, local bricks and hand-plastered white walls lend an authentic Thai charm to the entire resort. Here, 60 air-conditioned Superior Studios are swathed in crisp, white linen. They come with large, open living areas and semi-outdoor bathrooms so guests can enjoy the best of tropical nature in complete privacy. Also available are eight river-view Deluxe Studios as well as six Grand Deluxe Studios each appointed with an intimate double bathtub.

The resort's Pool Villas, situated right on the riverfront, are the height of luxury here. Lounge in your own private swimming pool and jacuzzi, whilst gazing out on panoramic views of the Mae Kok river. Or while away some lazy hours on a swing sofa in the tropical garden.

THIS PAGE (FROM TOP): Crisp whites, natural woods and a feeling of space pervade the Studios; the free-form pool blends in complete harmony with its natural environment.

OPPOSITE: Hedonism at its best— bask in the tropical sun, laze in the shade of the sala or take a dip—the Pool Villa presents many options for relaxation and recuperation.

...an oasis of luxury in an area that is rustically undeveloped...

In the evening, stroll to the Sala Rimnam Thai restaurant, which serves the best of local cuisine, or sample an array of authentic Italian dishes from every region of Italy at the Angellini Italian Restaurant. Waiting for your food to arrive is a special experience, as you watch the skilled chefs work their magic in the open kitchen. And, of course, each of their culinary creations is simply delicious.

At the resort's heart is the Chiang Saen Spa which has adapted ancient traditional Thai herbal treatments to offer a holistic approach to well-being. Using fresh herbs and essential oils from centuries-old recipes, the Spa pampers and soothes frazzled souls in an outdoor environment, close to nature.

Meanwhile, those seeking active pursuits can head to the ancient hilltop pagoda, Wat Phra That Doi Thung, or enjoy a scenic boat ride along the Mae Kok river. Golfers will find several spectacular courses nearby, while animal lovers can revel in elephant trekking. The night bazaar of Chiang Rai is always a hit, with a mind-boggling array of local goods, from mango wood accessories and wax paper lanterns to delicious local snacks. And if you really must mix business with pleasure, the resort has facilities such as an Internet corner and seminar room at your disposal. But perhaps with all this pampering, you will decide that indulgence, not work, is your priority.

FACTS		
ROOMS	60 superior studios • 8 deluxe studios • 6 grand deluxe studios • 4 pool villas	
FOOD	Sala Rim Nam Restaurant: Thai • Angellini Italian Restaurant: Italian	
DRINK	pool bar	
FEATURES	spa • seminar room • infinity-edge pool • Internet corner	
NEARBY	Mae Kok River • Wat Phra Kaew • Wat Phra That Doi Thung • Myanmar • Laos • elephant treks	
CONTACT	124/15 Kohloy Road, Tambon Robwiang, Amphur Muang, Chiang Rai 57000 • telephone: +62.53.910 400 • facsimile: +62.53.719 650 • email: info@thelegend-chiangrai.com • website: www.thelegend-chiangrai.com	

PHOTOGRAPHS COURTESY OF THE LEGEND CHIANG RAI.

Phu Chaisai Mountain Resort + Spa

Perched on a hillside near the famed Doi Mae Salong Mountain in the Chiang Rai province, Phu Chaisai Mountain Resort and Spa is an enchanting retreat. "Rustic yet sophisticated" is how this boutique resort has been described and indeed it is an apt, although contradictory, description.

From the outside, Phu Chaisai looks like a cluster of ordinary bamboo huts with thatched roofs—and in some ways, they are. Built humbly, as the hill-tribe people have done for centuries, the huts are made of everyday materials available in the area, such as bamboo and mud. But what make this collection of huts special are the things in and around them. Phu Chaisai's owners hail from the same family that have long been the decorators and builders of choice for the upper echelons of Thailand's society. Their talent for design and eye for aesthetics are immediately evident here.

The resort is appointed with all things natural—hammocks languidly hanging from ceilings; wooden and bamboo furniture and soft diaphanous sheets draped from the tops of four-poster beds. Every room is graced with a perfect view of the hillside and valley, and is equipped with all you need to stay in

THIS PAGE: *A sweeping vista across the hillside and sun-drenched terrace by the pool.*

OPPOSITE (FROM LEFT): *The dreamy ambience of a guestroom featuring a four-poster bed; lazy long lunches outdoors in the al fresco restaurant—celebrating a slower and kinder pace of life at Phu Chaisai.*

Every room is graced with a perfect view of the hillside and valley...

large community of ethnic Chinese people welcomes you with famous Yunnan cuisine and fragrant Chinese tea. After this satisfying meal, head to the colourful gardens in front of the Royal Villa for an energising walk before returning to Phu Chaisai to experience its excellent spa.

One of the unique things about Phu Chaisai's spa is the spectacular views of the valley through the picture-perfect windows of its three treatment rooms. Gaze at the woods at sunset while you enjoy a massage by the spa's dedicated staff, or enjoy a fragrant bath filled with local flowers, whilst surrounded by scented candles.

At the end of the day, enjoy dinner in the privacy of your own cottage, or head to the al fresco restaurant to dine on outstanding northern Thai specialties, made from the organic ingredients from Phu Chaisai's own farm. And after your moonlit meal, retire to your cottage for blissful dreams about this unforgettable place.

tune with nature. Guests are encouraged to revitalise themselves in the cool mountain air and to drink in the beauty of its outdoors in a myriad of ways.

Explore the countryside on mountain horses, take a cruise down the Kok river to witness the remote lifestyle of the local people, or go trekking on the marked trails that crisscross the expansive property. The resort can also arrange visits to the nearby Doi Mae Salong mountain range, where a

FACTS

ROOMS	10 superior rooms • 10 deluxe rooms • 10 executive suite cottages • 2 honeymoon suite cottages • 2 pool villas
FOOD	Phu View Restaurant & Bar: traditional Thai
DRINK	Phu View Restaurant & Bar
FEATURES	pool • spa • meeting and conference facilities • boutique • souvenir shop
NEARBY	Horseback riding • fishing • Chiang Saen • Golden Triangle • Doi Tung • Doi Mae Salong • rafting • Long Neck villages • Rong Khun Temple
CONTACT	388 Moo 4, Baan Mae Salong Nai Mae Chan, Chiang Rai 57110 • telephone: +66.53.918 6367 • facsimile: +66.53.918 333 • email: contact@phu-chaisai.com • website: www.phu-chaisai.com

PHOTOGRAPHS COURTESY OF PHU CHAISAI RESORT.

The Chedi Chiang Mai

Ultra-chic and unmistakably luxurious, The Chedi Chiang Mai is an icon of style set on the banks of the renowned Mae Ping river. Just 8 km (5 miles) away from Chiang Mai International Airport, it demonstrates good taste at every turn.

Tradition meets modernity in each of The Chedi's 84 exquisitely designed rooms and suites. Uncluttered and graceful fittings are intelligently matched with Asian art pieces, while teak and terrazzo accents give an urban feel. Each Deluxe Room is endowed with a spacious balcony offering spectacular views of the Mae Ping river and its surrounding mountain range, likely to take your breath away.

In the Chedi Club Suites, large sitting areas in muted tones with elegantly understated furnishings are the perfect place to relax or dine in style. In the evenings, enjoy a romantic dinner for two under the stars before snuggling up in the suites' exquisitely large and comfortable beds.

Dining is indeed a real treat at The Chedi—all favourites are listed in the room service menu, but it is the experience of dining at the hotel's delightful restaurant that is a sheer gastronomic delight. Simply

known as The Restaurant, it is set in a split-level colonial house that dates back to 1913, and serves a fabulous array of traditional northern Thai specialties, Pacific Rim cuisine and innovative Asian creations. An extensive wine list offers the perfect pairings with each dish, while private dining rooms can be booked for parties and grander affairs. And little guests never miss out—children are specially catered for, too.

To whet your appetite with an apéritif, head to The Bar, an intimate ground-floor terrace. Enjoy a light snack and refreshing drink at the Lobby Lounge before heading out on the town. But if you'd prefer a quiet night in, with a glass of great wine and a cigar, the cosy daybeds at the Terrace Bar may beckon. For business travellers, the Chedi Club Suites provide additional facilities, including access to the exclusive Chedi Club Lounge. All bars and lounges are equipped with wireless Internet access if you must keep pace with the outside world.

But if escapism is your thing, The Chedi Spa offers Thai massages, body scrubs, herbal baths and beauty treatments, in a serene environment of scented gardens and water features. And before leaving, visit The Chedi's exclusive Boutique to take home some fabulous signature products, Asian arts and enchanting memories.

THIS PAGE: The stylish Chedi Club Suites offer large spaces for lounging and relaxing

OPPOSITE (FROM TOP): Sumptuous colour schemes warm the suites' bathrooms; bold statements harmonise with delicate touches in the rooms.

PHOTOGRAPHS COURTESY OF THE CHEDI CHIANG MAI.

FACTS

ROOMS	52 rooms • 32 suites
FOOD	The Restaurant: Thai, international and Indian
DRINK	Terrace Bar and Cigar Lounge • The Bar • The Lobby Lounge
FEATURES	spa • pool • health club • boutique
NEARBY	river tours • elephant trekking • golf course
CONTACT	123 Charoen Prathet Road, T Changklan A Muang, Chiang Mai 50100 • telephone: +66.53.253 333 • facsimile: +66.53.253 352 • email: chedichiangmai@ghmhotels.com • website: www.ghmhotels.com

D2hotel chiang mai

Trendy meets traditional at D2hotel chiang mai. Part of the Dusit name, D2 unites international standards of hospitality with the uniquely Thai blend of service and style.

D2's location emphasises the hotel's philosophy of fusing traditional with modern. Located just off the famous Chang Klan Road, D2 is near to the bustling night bazaar and some of Chiang Mai's well-known cultural attractions.

Nearby is the Tapae Gateway, where the town's ancient temples stand. Inside D2, spacious interiors integrate natural materials to create a high-tech and functional living environment. The contemporary patterns of its charming rooms play up the organic assets of space and light. The lobby lounge was designed as a 'hyper-space'—a hip eclectic gallery of high-energy, high-contrast and high-activity. Bold design and strokes of

artwork energise the senses, reminding guests that the modernistic movement has arrived in Chiang Mai.

Accordingly, the sexy, modern design of D2's rooms incorporates high-speed Internet access, modem and fax data port connections and dual phone lines complete with voice mail. Panoramic flat TV screens show the latest movies, TV programmes and news bulletins on cable.

...the modernistic movement has arrived in Chiang Mai.

Devarana Spa is D2's award-winning place to go for relaxation. The word Devarana, meaning 'garden in heaven', is derived from a piece of ancient Thai literature, *Tribhumphraruang*, and the poetry of the language is what inspired the concept of this spa. Continually innovating and introducing new treatments, the Devarana aims to create the best ever spa experience for its lucky guests.

Featuring five private treatment rooms—one grand suite, three double suites and one single deluxe—the Devarana Spa's décor is uniquely designed to feel like a celestial garden. Each spacious suite is elegantly decorated in contemporary Thai style and beautifully equipped with distinctively Thai spa amenities.

Guests at the Devarana Spa can enjoy a superb variety of pampering treatments in a stress-relieving environment, including massage, beauty treatment, water treatment, facials, and special packages, all delivered with exceptional Thai service. The spa's signature treatments—Devarana bath, Devarana massage and Devarana scrub—are particularly outstanding for their sensational effects and de-stressing benefits. In addition to individual treatments, the spa offers several special programmes and an annual membership option, representing excellent value for regular spa-goers.

When you are fully relaxed and done with pampering, enjoy a swim at the hotel's outdoor pool, burn up some energy at its state-of-the-art health club, or head out to take in the nearby sights. D2's effective and efficient concierges are always close at hand to help guests select activities and arrange for transportation to nearby hotspots like the elephant work camps, butterfly and orchid farms, hill tribe villages and spectacular national parks.

THIS PAGE: *Fiery oranges, warm yellows and rich browns provide a welcoming feel to the rooms.*
OPPOSITE: *Metropolitan and contemporary, D2 offers a stylish and comfortable gateway to the bright lights of downtown Chiang Mai.*

Dinner comes highly recommended at the hotel's quirky yet sophisticated restaurant, Moxie, which serves an exciting selection of international modern cuisine. Behind the playfully chic dining space, Moxie's experienced chefs regularly innovate a selection of traditional recipes to create haute-style food with a touch of Eastern exoticism. Choose accompanying wine from a stunning worldwide collection in the ceiling-high glass shelves and admire the woven rattan sculpture wall above the buffet station. Or drink in the atmosphere at the Mix Bar, a stylish lounge replete with sleek leather armchairs, sumptuous fabrics and muted beige tones. Watch Chiang Mai's hip crowd wander through D2's social gathering area to the best of lounge music.

D2's original Siam Soul Thai lounge music is a new genre created solely for D2hotel chiang mai. The fusion of modern Western lounge music with traditional Thai instrumentation and themes will fill your soul and have you coming back for more.

D2 also boasts one boardroom and two event rooms with a pre-function area and a break-out room—ideal for those essential breaks between important

discussions. This is the perfect venue for small seminars, regional meetings and medium-sized conferences, complemented by the hotel's high-tech meeting equipment and the tasteful, contemporary interiors which exude a sense of effortless chic.

When business is over and the pleasure begins, D2 still remains the venue of choice, in an area where old meets new and where service meets style. Just a five-minute walk from Chiang Mai city centre, the funky downtown location of D2 ensures that its guests are at the very heart of where it's happening. And when you're tired of living and breathing the vibrance of Chang Mai, D2 provides an elegant yet homely escape.

FACTS		
	ROOMS	130 guestrooms and suites
	FOOD	Moxie: modern international
	DRINK	Mix Bar
	FEATURES	outdoor pool • health club • banquet/conference/meeting facilities • Devarana Spa • Internet access
	NEARBY	Chiang Mai night bazaar • Tapae Gateway • elephant work camp
	CONTACT	100 Chang Klan Road, Amphur Muang, Chiang Mai 50100 • telephone: +66 53 999 999 • facsimile: +66 53 999 900 • email: d2chotel@dusit.com • website: www.d2hotels.com

Four Seasons Resort Chiang Mai

Tucked away in the breathtakingly scenic Mae Rim Valley is the beautiful Four Seasons Resort Chiang Mai. Gorgeous landscaped gardens and emerald paddy fields surround its 64 luxurious Pavilion Rooms. Richly decorated in Lanna-style golds and maroons, each features its own bedroom, sitting room and private sala.

For families or friends holidaying together, the resort offers a host of Residences that combine the signature Four Seasons comfort and service with the exclusiveness of a private home. These Residences are available in one-, two-, or three-bedroom configurations, with private terraces and plunge pools. The three-bedroom Penthouse Residences occupy two levels joined by a teak spiral staircase, with stunning views of the nearby mountains and countryside. During the cool season, snuggle up by the fireplace—a fixture in every Residence—and enjoy meals prepared by your very own housekeeper.

Explore the resort's lush grounds, where you will meet the resident family of water buffalo. As the sun sets, the same paths take on a magical glow with rustic torches and beautiful oversized lanterns. Or learn to cook at the resort's famed cooking school, where guests can choose from a six-day programme or select from individual modules. Situated in a spacious and well-

...Four Seasons comfort and service with the exclusiveness of a private home.

THIS PAGE (FROM TOP): *Rice paddies and majestic mountains—Four Seasons Resort Chiang Mai's peaceful landscape; relax in a sala at the spa.*
OPPOSITE: *Spacious Pavilion Rooms in Lanna style offer lush views of the tranquil surrounds.*

equipped pavilion, the cooking school reveals the secrets of classic Thai dishes, like Paad Thai and Tom Yam Goong.

For indulgence, the resort's spa awaits. A palatial three-storey villa, the spa was designed in the Lanna style and inspired by a northern Thai temple. Within its seven stunning treatment suites, guests may enjoy therapies drawn from ancient Thai rituals to beautify, relax and heal.

Within 10 minutes of the resort are a myriad of sights and activities. See an endless variety of exotic blooms at the Sanamphung Orchid Farm, or explore a nearby butterfly farm. Picnic by the Mae Sa Waterfalls, take a slow ride on an elephant at the Mae Sa Elephant Camp or play golf at the scenic Chiang Mai Green Valley Golf and Country Club.

Later on, savour delectable Thai cuisine at the resort's Sala Mae Rim restaurant or in the comfort of your private sala. Then sit back and relax in the serenity of the Four Seasons Resort Chiang Mai.

FACTS		
	ROOMS	64 pavilions • 16 residences
	FOOD	Sala Mae Rim: Thai • Terraces: international
	DRINK	Elephant Bar
	FEATURES	spa • health club • yoga barn• library • cooking school • banquet facilities • tennis • conference facilities
	NEARBY	Sainamphung Orchid Farm • Mae Sa Waterfalls • Mae Sa Elephant Camp • Chiang Mai Green Valley Golf and Country Club
	CONTACT	Mae Rim-Samoeng Old Road, Mae Rim, Chiang Mai 50180 • telephone: +66.53.298 181 • facsimile: +66.53.298 189 • email: reservations.chiangmai@fourseasons.com • website: www.fourseasons.com/chiangmai

PHOTOGRAPHS COURTESY OF FOUR SEASONS RESORT CHIANG MAI.

Mandarin Oriental Dhara Dhevi

Built to serve as a 'living museum', the Mandarin Oriental Dhara Dhevi has the honour of being the most ambitious resort in Asia. This stunning re-creation of the Lanna kingdom (AD 1296 to 1558) has been described as cultural immersion in the highest style. Spread over 24.2 ha (60 acres), the US$120 million resort is flanked by fortified walls and moats, a watch tower and a ceremonial lawn. At its heart, 123 ultra-chic villas and suites represent more than 20 different decorative approaches.

A stroll around its sprawling grounds reveals the resort as a veritable small city. Various eras and regions are amazingly depicted, from medieval Chiang Mai to

colonial Burma. Mandarin Oriental Dhara Dhevi is modelled on a royal village, with a palace, market, prayer hall, villas for nobility, rice barns, farming villages, vegetable gardens and lotus ponds, all of which are tended to and occupied by scores of farmers, artisans, villagers and merchants.

Getting around this vast resort comes with its own measure of old-world grandeur and charm. Guests are taken to their villas in glittering horse-drawn carriages or antique samlors, to the tinkling tunes of xylophones.

Its owners have spared no expense in recreating life as it was centuries ago, and its young architect, Rachen Intawong, worked tirelessly to achieve true authenticity. Intawong explored the northern countryside on his Vespa, studying details large and small, from farming tools and prayer offerings to doorframes, temples and barns. These details were then woven

into Mandarin Oriental Dhara Dhevi's construction, to give it the form of a living, breathing city.

The design of the pavilions employs the style of traditional high-gabled Thai homes, making extensive use of the region's polished teak wood. Meanwhile, its villas borrow their unique barrel-shape from one- and two-storey northern Thai rice barns. Charming forest animals and birds carved tenderly out of wood appear in the rich detailing.

Mandarin Oriental Dhara Dhevi's residences are designed in the Mandalay style with 19th-century English furnishings, magnificent chandeliers, heavy drapes and trompe-l'oeil walls. Its Colonial Suites are similarly inspired by British empire chic, with plush divans and high ceilings, and spacious balconies or direct access to the exotic garden.

For more opulent Thai style, check into Mandarin Oriental Dhara Dhevi's grand deluxe villas, which have received rapturous

reviews. In his esteemed Hideaway Report, a newsletter for high-end travellers, Andrew Harper called it 'some of the most lavish accommodations we have ever encountered'. Hardly surprising—Dhara Dhevi's private plunge pools and whirlpool tubs overlook fertile rice paddies, and its Thai-style villas are composed of teak floors and sculptural yet traditional sloping ceilings, offsetting a selection of antique and contemporary furnishings.

This extravagant décor is highlighted with the use of hand-woven Thai silk fabrics and marble trim. Juxtaposing the very old against the very new, Mandarin Oriental Dhara Dhevi surrounds its guests with genuine antiques, yet keeps them connected to the outside world through state-of-the-art communications and entertainment systems.

To allow guests to experience the lifestyles of Thai monarchs, Mandarin Oriental Dhara Dhevi has fashioned three themed suites and a villa—namely, the Spa Penthouse Suite, Dhara Devi Suite, Chiang Mai Suite and the Royal Villa.

Measuring 373 sq m (3,990 sq ft), the Spa Penthouse Suite was inspired by the royal palace at the Mandalay court. Besides a living room, dining room, pantry and bedroom, the suite's special feature is its

THIS PAGE: The Dheva Spa evokes classical elegance in white marble, with subtle Thai accents in its decorative finishes.

OPPOSITE: Based on a Burmese palace, the external spires, sculptures and statues of the Dheva Spa are truly awe-inspiring.

private spa, with luxurious treatment and exercise rooms so guests can enjoy their spa services in complete privacy.

But if you are seeking enlightenment by being closer to the gods, then the Dhara Dhevi Suite certainly raises the level of luxe to dizzying heights. Its palace structure towers 22 m (72 ft) above ground and employs traditional northern Thai and Burmese styles. Lie back on the suite's original Thai-style King bed and survey the panoramic view of your 'kingdom'.

Cultural exploration is key to the entire experience. Guides love showing curious guests around the resort, and can explain everything from the origins of the buildings, to the symbolism of various murals, wood carvings and frescoed ceilings. Wizened old women from nearby villages practise their weaving, basketry and woodcarving at the Mandarin Oriental Dhara Dhevi craft village, providing a glimpse into the traditional local folk arts. While these ladies will happily provide lessons to willing adults,

children too may experience Thai life through Mandarin Oriental Dhara Dhevi's Lanna Kid's Club. The activities on offer never fail to please, ranging from ever-popular water buffalo rides and fun handicrafts, to basic Thai language tuition and Thai dance classes.

Learn to play a game of *takraw* (Thai volleyball); unravel the mystery of creating a Thai jungle curry; or plant rice alongside farmers in the field to gain a firsthand appreciation of this backbreaking work.

Mandarin Oriental Dhara Dhevi's mission of 'edification, not just mere indulgence' is also played out in the form of a library that stocks 5,000 tomes on Asian culture, as well as other reading materials, CDs and DVDs on a wide range of subjects. Lovers of the arts will feel privileged to have access to a 250-seat amphitheatre where dramatic, musical and dance performances are regularly staged.

But if you prefer a more leisurely, indulgent holiday, the nexus of Mandarin Oriental Dhara Dhevi, the Dheva Spa, might be more to your taste. Like a mirage on the property's secluded grounds, this magnificent teak palace stands regal, watching over a grey granite courtyard.

A spectacular re-creation of a 19th-century Burmese palace, the Dheva Spa unfolds over 3,066 sq m (33,000 sq ft), with 25 treatment suites and rooms to pamper, heal and restore even the most world-weary of souls. Capped by a seven-tier roof—symbolic of the seven steps to Nirvana—every inch of the spa is adorned with ornate mouldings and sculptures depicting animals and Buddhist motifs, based on the Burmese original in Mandalay, Myanmar. Its breathtaking exterior is matched by its beautiful interiors. Within these carefully sculpted walls, guests can find their bliss in a wonderful blend of Oriental and international therapies, employing ancient secrets of herbal remedies and holistic techniques. Some therapies have ancient origins dating back over 4,000 years, and were practised in the Lanna kingdom in centuries past.

Indeed, amongst its white marble courtyards and dark wood pavilions, guests are transported back to a time when rituals and ceremonies were a part of daily life. In those days, spiritual awareness was considered key to physical and mental well-being. These same beliefs hold true at

the Dheva Spa, where a tiny bell chimes to welcome guests as they are escorted through its grand reception.

An extensive spa menu offers treatments unique to Thailand, as well as relaxation rituals indigenous to northern Lanna culture. In keeping with the spa's heritage, guests often opt for The Lanna Signature Ceremony, to experience some of Chiang Mai's ancient beauty rituals. First is a herbal footbath infused with a local healing herb, then a

luxurious herbal bath for the body. Next is the Oriental Body Glow treatment, and an exquisite body wrap using another Lanna ingredient to awaken and refresh the skin. Finally, experience the Tok Sen, a stimulating Lanna massage technique once popular in northern Thailand, but which is rarely practised outside of the Dheva Spa today.

To complement its rituals and treatments, the spa offers a menu of wholesome delights, created by executive sous chef

Fabrizio Aceti. Hailing from northern Italy, chef Aceti has designed a selection of seasonal dishes that each contain between 420 and 1600 kilojoules (100 and 380 calories). Each item carries useful details of its nutritional breakdown so health-conscious guests are always aware of what—and how much of it—passes their lips. Wherever possible, ingredients used by the spa are certified 100 per cent organic and produced locally in the nurseries at The Royal Project, north of Chiang Mai.

On the subject of food, dining at this resort is also one of its guests' greatest pleasures. The Mandarin Oriental Dhara Dhevi boasts a range of superb restaurants that specialise in different culinary themes. The delicious diversity of Thai cuisine is offered at Le Grand Lanna, set in a cluster of traditional two-storey buildings. Fujian serves authentic Chinese cuisine in an elegant Sino-Portuguese-style mansion. Fine French food with a Mediterranean touch can be enjoyed at Farang Ses, in a gorgeous Thai teak pavilion overlooking the paddy fields. For satisfying breakfasts and all-day dining, the resort's Rice Terrace, serving international cuisine, is a great option.

Down by the resort's swimming pool, sun loungers are laid out with water spritzers. Sip on chilled bottles of water as you sink into your chair and soak up the glorious tropical weather. Of course, the holiday poolside experience is undeniably enhanced with stronger drinks, and the bartenders here concoct them brilliantly. Ginger martinis, mangosteen mojitos, and fresh lime sodas over crushed ice and sugar are just the thing to beat the heat, so let there be no holding back on your part.

For those with a penchant for retail therapy, visit Kad Dhara in the resort—a small village-style group of 19th-century-style shophouses mirroring the style of those found in Chiang Mai of old. The shophouses are home to nearly 30 different boutiques and local designer shops selling Thai and Laotian silks, cashmere, art, antiques, old photographs, books and jewellery.

As night falls, torches spring to life, beckoning pretty fireflies to flicker against the halos of light. As Mandarin Oriental Dhara Dhevi's busy team of farmers, merchants and caretakers retire at dusk, they leave its grounds to creatures of the night—crickets,

cicadas and nocturnal birds—who play a symphony of nature's music. This is the evening cue for gastronomical pleasures to begin. Later, with appetites satiated, guests invariably retire to their villas or suites to slumber in the peace, quiet and luxury of a true Thai kingdom.

THIS PAGE: The welcoming glow of Le Grand Lanna, set amidst winding pathways and manicured gardens.
OPPOSITE: Intricate inlaid woodwork doors and glowing Chinese lanterns give the Fujian restaurant its cosy ambience.

FACTS		
ROOMS	123 villas and suites	
FOOD	Le Grand Lanna: Thai • Fujian: Chinese • Farang Ses: fine French • Rice Terrace: international • Loy Kham Bar: snacks • Akaligo: international	
DRINK	Loy Kham Bar • Lobby Bar	
FEATURES	Dheva Spa • health and fitness centre • cultural centre • amphitheatre • cooking classes • Lanna Kid's Club • Kad Dhara shopping village • library	
NEARBY	Chiang Mai night bazaar • Doi Inthanon National Park • Wat Chedi Luang	
CONTACT	51/4 Chiang Mai-Sankampaeng Road, Moo 1 T. Tasala, A. Muang, Chiang Mai 50000 • telephone: +66.53.888 888 • facsimile: +66.53.888 999 • email: mocnx-reservations@mohg.com • website: www.mandarinoriental.com	

PHOTOGRAPHS BY PHOOM NARISCHAT, COURTESY OF MANDARIN ORIENTAL DHARA DHEVI.

Rachamankha Hotel

Created by two of Thailand's most renowned designers and architects, Rachmankha is more a treasury of old Lanna culture than simply a hotel. Lanna artwork and Chinese antiquities abound in every room and space, along with unique pieces from Burma and Laos.

No expense was spared, nor was any detail ignored, in constructing and decorating Rachamankha. For architect Ong-ard Satrabandhu and designer Rooj Changtrakul, this labour of love transcends the bottom line.

Modelled after the viharn or 'chapel' of one of Thailand's most beautiful temples—the Wat Phra That Lampang Luang in the Lampang province—this 24-room, single-storey inn is a neat assemblage of white plaster buildings capped by peaked terracotta roofs. To reflect its roots in Thai architecture, the hotel was planned according to ancient building principles.

At its heart are two manicured courtyards, rich with flowering trees and an open-air pavilion decorated with plush white couches, pots of vibrant flowers, and antique Thai artwork. Peace reigns here despite Rachamanhka's location just off Chiang Mai's main thoroughfare.

Thick walls covered with white limestone plaster keep the rooms invitingly cool. Large and comfortable, the rooms

Rachamankha is more a treasury of old Lanna culture than simply a hotel.

THIS PAGE *(FROM TOP)*: *Lanna-style lanterns lend a warm glow to the spacious interior of The Restaurant; the architecture of the hotel incorporates ancient Asian design principles.*

OPPOSITE: *A plush guestroom, with antique artwork and rich red cushions, pays homage to history, whilst also keeping a sophisticated, modern feel.*

each differ slightly in décor, thanks to the antique furnishings: old Lanna-style doors with ornate handles, table lamps of delicate Chinese porcelain, and charming lanterns with dangling tassels.

A teal-tiled pool inspires contemplation, while a handsome library of art and history books could keep Rachamankha's guests entertained for days. A huge cloth painting depicting the life of Lord Buddha presides over The Restaurant. Here, traditional Thai cuisine is served alongside a selection of

dishes that combine the flavours of Vietnam, Japan and Europe. After your meal, adjourn to The Bar, decorated with a rare Chinese antique liqueur screen and lithographs by early 20th-century painters.

So chic and well-designed is this hotel that it made the *Conde Nast Traveller* 2005 Hot List—less than a year after it opened. It certainly is no mean feat, yet one would expect nothing less of an establishment that was created through a passion for culture and excellent design.

FACTS

ROOMS	2 two-bedroom suites • 4 deluxe rooms • 18 superior rooms
FOOD	The Restaurant: Northern Thai and European
DRINK	The Bar
FEATURES	pool • library
NEARBY	Wat Phra Singh
CONTACT	6 Rachamankha 9, T Phra Singh A Muang, Chiang Mai 50200 • telephone: +66.53.904 111/2/3 • facsimile: +66.53.904 114 • email: reservations@rachamankha.com • website: www.rachamankha.com

PHOTOGRAPHS COURTESY OF RACHAMANKA HOTEL.

Baan Saen Doi Spa

Hidden in the foothills of the Suthep-Pui mountain range, just 20 minutes west of Chiang Mai, Baan Saen Doi is a luxurious spa destination laid out like a tasteful holiday home. Privacy and exclusivity are the buzzwords here—there are three gorgeous suites, each with its own theme, and named after famous local mountains.

Both spa and design enthusiasts will find plenty to fawn over. This Lanna-style private villa was designed by architect Adul Heranya and interior designer Yutthana Mohprasit, who were inspired by the hill tribes of the surrounding region. This is apparent in the decorative accents in each room—lamps with coils looped around their bases, suggestive of the long-necked Karen tribes; chairs with leggings reminiscent of the style of the Akha tribe; and black pillows, conveying the Vietnamese and Southern Chinese features of the Yao tribe, strategically strewn about on sofas throughout the house.

The mainstays of hill-tribe life—pressed aluminium and bamboo—are also used to great effect. They frame doorways and form much of the furniture, providing a solid backdrop against which everyday tools like musical instruments, fabric patterns, dress and colour serve as decorative elements.

Owner Wanphen Sakdatorn's emphasis on keeping things simple and uncluttered is evident in the elegant use of dark woods accented by neat green foliage and a few well-placed white orchids. Each airy room in the house is awash in sunlight, thanks to its high ceilings and the generous use of glass.

...there are three gorgeous suites, each with its own theme.

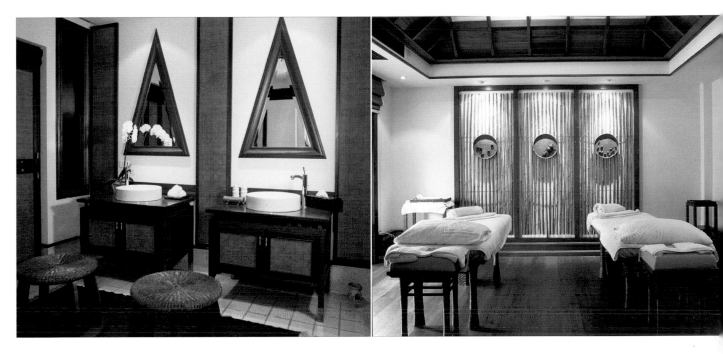

While the interior decoration deserves full marks for evoking a sense of peace and relaxation, it is Baan Saen Doi's renowned spa services that people flock here for. Warm, genial and impeccably professional, the staff is always on hand to make guests feel at home. Sit down to a chilled glass of tamarind juice as your host helps you choose a programme to suit both your lifestyle and budget.

Each treatment begins with time spent unwinding in the steam room, where a glass roof allows you, depending on the time of day, to look up to the sunlit sky or the stars.

Guests are then led to one of the treatment rooms to experience a range of exquisite body or beauty treatments, including body polishes, shiatsu, Swedish massage and reflexology—all to rejuvenate and relax.

All Baan Saen Doi's staff was trained at the renowned Chiva Som Academy in Bangkok. And it truly shows—they are wonderfully adept at both Eastern and Western techniques. That said, Baan Saen Doi prides itself on being the only spa in northern Thailand to offer hot stone massages, which also happens to be the favourite treatment among guests here.

THIS PAGE (FROM LEFT): Decorative motifs in the lobby, such as long neck lamps and ceiling patterns, reflect the inspiration drawn from local hill tribes.
OPPOSITE: Each room, including the foyer, basks in natural light. Water features add to the tranquillity.

This unparalleled experience connects the body with nature through its wondrous mineral properties. Various stones are heated under an electric blanket—think jasper, jade, aventurine and carnelian. When warmed, the therapist cradles the stones in her hands one by one, dips them in almond oil and massages them against the body. The deep massage allows each stone to release its mineral magic, while assisting the body in absorbing the stones' healing properties through the circulatory and muscular systems. The result is a splendid feeling of released stress, better blood circulation and improved muscle tone. End the treatment with an

THIS PAGE (FROM LEFT): *The generous bathroom of the Master Suite; an oil painting by Chiang Mai artist, Vichit Chaivong, adds to the welcoming warmth of the Master Suite.*

OPPOSITE: *Relax on a lounger on the spacious veranda.*

Indian-style head massage, in which the therapist curls and pulls the hair and earlobes, while massaging deeply into the curvatures of the face and skull. This invigorating treatment provides a refreshing jolt to awaken the senses from the dreamy state of the hot stone massage therapy.

Meals can be taken at the nearby Saenham Terrace Restaurant, where a delectable menu of classic central and northern Thai dishes is on offer to whet appetites. The restaurant looks out to the swimming pool encircled by flourishing plants, enhancing the resort's tranquillity.

The pleasures of Baan Saen Doi continue in each room. Its comfortable beds beckon you to laze in. And its bathrooms are nothing short of palatial. A giant tub takes pride of place and invites its residents to sink in for a languorous soak before drifting to bed amid the quiet, soothing sounds of nature. It's time to spoil yourself at Baan Saen Doi, far, far away from the stress of life.

PHOTOGRAPHS COURTESY OF BAAN SAEN DOI SPA.

FACTS

ROOMS	3 suites
FOOD	Saenkham Terrace Restaurant: central and northern Thai
DRINK	dining room • lobby • Saenkham Terrace Restaurant
FEATURES	spa
NEARBY	Chiang Mai
CONTACT	199/135 Moo 3 Baan Nai Fun 2, Kan Klong Chonprathan Road T. Mae-Hia, A. Muang Chiang Mai 50100 • telephone: +66.53.839 260 • facsimile: +66.53.838 993 • email: info@baansaendoi.com • website: www.baansaendoi.com

index

Numbers in *italics* denote pages where pictures appear. Numbers in **bold** denote map pages.

index

index

picturecredits

The publisher would like to thank the following for permission to reproduce their photographs:

Anantara Resort + Spa Koh Samui 4-5, 109 (top)
Anantara Resort + Spa Hua Hin front cover: towels, 114 (below)
Bed Supperclub 41
Cedric Arnold back cover: lotus, 8-9, 17 (top), 22 (top right and top), 23-27, 30 (left), 31 (below), 40, 42-43, 57 (centre), 58 (top right), 116
The Chedi Chiang Mai front cover: bed, 188 (top)
Costa Lanta, Krabi back flap, 123
Dave Lloyd 49, 111 (below), 112-113, 118 (top), 120 (top), 122, 200 (below)
Fabrizio Aceti 19 (centre and below), 39 (centre)
Four Seasons Resort Chiang Mai 199 (below)
Hans Fonk/The Jim Thompson Thai Silk Company 36 (below)
i.sawan Residential Spa + Club front cover: water lily and bamboo

Kirimaya Golf Resort and Spa back flap
Luca Invernizzi Tettoni 2, 6, 13-16, 17 (below), 18, 20-21, 22 (below), 28-29, 30 (right), 31 (top), 32 (top), 33-35, 36 (top), 37 (below), 38 (top), 39 (top and below), 44-48, 50-53, 54 (below), 55-56, 57 (top and below), 58 (top left and below), 59, 106-108, 110, 111 (top), 114 (top), 115, 117 (below), 118 (below), 119, 124 (top), 180-187, 188 (below), 189-198, 200 (top), 201
Luca Invernizzi Tettoni/The Jim Thompson Thai Silk Company 37 (top), 109 (below), 121,
Luca Invernizzi Tettoni/The Oriental Hotel 38 (below)
Mandarin Oriental Dhara Dhevi front flap
Reinhard Dirscherl/Tips Images 124 (below), 125
SALA Samui Resort + Spa 117 (top)
Scott A Woodward Photography 120
Shari Kessler 12, 19 (top), 32 (below), 54 (top)

directory

Amari Emerald Cove Resort
88/8 Moo 4, Tambol Koh Chang,
King Amphur, Koh Chang 23170
telephone : +66.39.552 000
facsimile : +66.39.552 001
emeraldcove@amari.com
www.amari.com

Amari Trang Beach Resort
199 Moo 5 Had Pak Meng,
Changlang Road, Changlang Beach,
Tambon Maifad, Amphur Sikao,
Trang 92150
telephone : +66.75.205.888
facsimile : +66.75.205 899
trangbeach@amari.com
www.amari.com

Anantara Resort + Spa Koh Samui
99/9 Moo 1 Bo Phut Bay, Koh Samui,
Surat Thani 84320
telephone : +66.77.428 300
facsimile : +66.77.428 310
infosamui@anantara.com
www.anantara.com

Baan Saen Doi Spa
199/135 Moo 3 Baan Nai Fun 2,
Kan Klong Chonprathan Road T. Mae-Hia,
A. Muang Chiang Mai 50100
telephone : +66.53.839 260
facsimile : +66.53.838 993
info@baansaendoi.com
www.baansaendoi.com

The Baan Thai Wellness Retreat
7 Soi Sukhumvit 32, Sukhumvit Road,
Klongton, Klongtoey, Bangkok 10110
telephone : +66.2.258 5403
facsimile : +66.2.258 9517
contact@thebaanthai.com
www.thebaanthai.com

Banyan Tree Phuket
33 Moo 4 Srisoonthorn Road, Cherngtalay,
Amphur Talang, Phuket 83110
telephone : +66.76.324 374
facsimile : +66.76.324 375
phuket@banyantree.com
www.banyantree.com

Bed Supperclub
26 Sukhumvit Soi 11, Sukhumvit Road,
Klongoey-Nua, Wattana, Bangkok 10110
telephone : +66.2.651 3537
facsimile : +66.2.651 3538
info@bedsupperclub.com
www.bedsupperclub.com

The Chedi Chiang Mai
123 Charoen Prathet Road,
T Changklan A Muang,
Chiang Mai 50100
telephone : +66.53.253 333
facsimile : +66.53.253 352
chedichiangmai@ghmhotels.com
www.ghmhotels.com

Conrad Bangkok
87 Wireless Road, Bangkok 10330
telephone : +66.2.690 9999
facsimile : +66.2.690 9000
info@conradbangkok.com
www.conradhotels.com

Costa Lanta, Krabi
Bangkok reservation office,
12/24 Sukhumvit Soi 33,
Bangkok 10110
telephone : +66.2.662 3550
facsimile : +66.2.260 9067
info@costalanta.com
www.costalanta.com

D2hotel chiang mai
100 Chang Klan Road, Amphur Muang,
Chiang Mai 50100
telephone : +66 53 999 999
facsimile : +66 53 999 900
d2chotel@dusit.com
www.d2hotels.com

Dusit Resort, Hua Hin
1349 Petchkasem Road, Cha-Am,
Phetchaburi 76120
telephone : +66.32.520 009/442 100
facsimile : +66.32.520 296
dcp@dusit.com
www.huahin.dusit.com

Dusit Resort, Pattaya
240/2 Pattaya Beach Road,
Pattaya City, Chonburi
telephone : +66.38.425 611-7
facsimile : +66.38.428 239
pattaya@dusit.com
www.dusit.com

The Dusit Thani, Bangkok
946 Rama IV Road,
Bangkok 10500
telephone : +66.22.009 000
facsimile : +66.22.366 400
dusitbkk@dusit.com
www.dusit.com

Emporium Suites
622 Sukhumvit Road, Klongton, Klongtoey,
Bangkok 10110
telephone : +66.2.664 9999
facsimile : +66.2.664 9990
info@emporiumsuites.com
www.emporiumsuites.com

**Evason Hideaway + Six Senses Spa
at Hua Hin**
9/22 Moo 5 Paknampran Beach, Pranburi,
Prachuap Khiri Khan 77220
telephone : +66.32.618 200
facsimile : +66.32.618 201
reservations-huahin@evasonhideaways.com
www.sixsenses.com/hideaway-huahin

Evason Hua Hin Resort + Six Senses Spa
9 Moo 3 Paknampran Beach, Pranburi,
Prachuap Khiri Khan, 77220
telephone : +66.32.632 111
facsimile : +66.32.632 112
reservations-huahin@evasonresorts.com
www.sixsenses.com/evason-huahin

Evason Phuket Resort + Six Senses Spa
100 Vised Road, Moo 2,
Tambol Rawai, Muang District,
Phuket 83100
telephone : +66.76.381 010
facsimile : +66.76.381 018
reservations-phuket@evasonresorts.com
www.sixsenses.com/evason-phuket

Face
29 Soi 38 Sukhumwit Rd,
Phrakhanong, Klongtoey,
Bangkok 10110
telephone : +66.27.186.048
facsimile : +66.27.186.047
ravi@facebars.com
www.facebars.com

Four Seasons Hotel Bangkok
155 Rajadamri Road, Bangkok 10330
telephone : +66.2.250.1000
facsimile : +66.2.254.5391
reservations.bangkok@fourseasons.com
www.fourseasons.com/bangkok

Four Seasons Resort Chiang Mai
Mae Rim-Samoeng Old Road,
Mae Rim, Chiang Mai 50180
telephone : +66.53.298 181
facsimile : +66.53.298 189
reservations.chiangmai@fourseasons.com
www.fourseasons.com/chiangmai

i.sawan Residential Spa + Club
5th floor, Grand Hyatt Erawan Bangkok,
494 Rajdamri Road, Bangkok 10330
telephone : +66.2.254 6310
facsimile : +66.2.254 6283
isawan.ghbangkok@hyattintl.com
www.bangkok.grand.hyatt.com

The Jim Thompson House
6 Kasemsan Soi 2, Rama 1 Road,
Bangkok 10330
telephone : +66 22.167 368
facsimile : +66 26 12 3744
supicha@jimthompsonhouse.com
www.jimthompsonhouse.com

Jim Thompson Retail Stores + Restaurants
96 Soi Peungmee 29, Bangchak,
Prakanong, Bangkok 10260
Thompson Bar and Restaurant:
Jim Thompson House Museum:
6 Soi Kasemsan 2, Rama 1 Road,
Bangkok 10330
Saladaeng Café:
120/1 Saladaeng Soi 1, Silom Road,
Bangkok 10500
Café 9:
9 Surawong Road, Bangkok 10500
telephone : +66 2762 2600
facsimile : +66 2762 2609
office@jimthompson.com
www.jimthompson.com

Kirimaya Golf Resort + Spa
1/3 Moo 6 Thanarat Road Moo-Si,
Pakchong Nakhon Ratchasima 30130
telephone : +66.44.426 000/099
facsimile : +66.44.929 888
book@kirimaya.com
www.kirimaya.com

Lamont Antiques + Contemporary Shops
3rd Floor, Gaysorn Plaza, 999,
Ploenchit Road, Bangkok 10330
Lamont Collections: The Oriental Hotel,
48 Oriental Avenue, Bangkok 10500
Lamont Phuket: 2G The Plaza Surin, 5/50
Moo 3, Chern Talay, Phuket 83110
telephone : +66.2.656 1392
facsimile : +66.2.656 1251
enquiries@lamont-design.com
www.lamont-design.com

The Legend Chiang Rai
124/15 Kohloy Road, Tambon Robwiang,
Amphur Muang, Chiang Rai 57000
telephone : +62.53.910 400
facsimile : +62.53.719 650
info@thelegend-chiangrai.com
www.thelegend-chiangrai.com

Mandarin Oriental Dhara Dhevi
51/4 Chiang Mai-Sankampaeng Road,
Moo 1 T. Tasala, A. Muang,
Chiang Mai 50000
telephone : +66.53.888 888
facsimile : +66.53.888 999
mocnx-reservations@mohg.com
www.mandarinoriental.com

The Mayfair Marriott Executive Apartments
60 Soi Langsuan, Lumpini, Pathumwan,
Bangkok 10330
telephone : +66.22.639 333
facsimile : +66.22.639 300
www.marriott.com/bkker

The Oriental Hotel
48 Oriental Avenue,
Bangkok 10500
telephone : +66.2.659 9000
facsimile : +66.2.659 0000
orbkk-reservations@mohg.com
www.mandarinoriental.com

The Paradise Koh Yao Beach Resort + Spa
24 Moo 4, Tambol Koh Yao Noi,
Amphur Koh Yao,
Phang Nga 82160
telephone : +66.1.892 4878
facsimile : +66.76.238 913
info@theparadise.biz
www.theparadise.biz

Phu Chaisai Mountain Resort + Spa
388 Moo 4,
Baan Mae Salong Nai Mae Chan,
Chiang Rai 57110
telephone : +66.53.918 6367
facsimile : +66.53.918 333
contact@phu-chaisai.com
www.phu-chaisai.com

Pimalai Resort + Spa
99 Moo 5, Ban Kan Tiang Beach,
Koh Lanta, Krabi 81150
telephone : +66.75.607 999
facsimile : +66.75.607 998
reservation@pimalai.com
www.pimalai.com

Rachamanka Hotel
6 Rachamankha 9,
T Phra Singh A Muang,
Chiang Mai 50200
telephone : +66.53.904 111/2/3
facsimile : +66.53.904 114
reservations@rachamankha.com
www.rachamankha.com

Rayavadee
214 Moo 2, Tambol Ao-Nang,
Amphur Muang, Krabi 81000
telephone : +66.75.620 740-3
facsimile : +66.75.620 630
reservation@rayavadee.com
www.rayavadee.com

SALA Samui Resort + Spa
10/9 Moo 5, Baan Plai Laem, Bophut,
Koh Samui, Suratthani 84320
telephone : +66.77.245 888
facsimile : +66.77.245 889
info@salasamui.com
www.salasamui.com

Sareerarom Tropical Spa
117 Thong Lo Road, 10, Sukhumvit 55,
Wattana, Bangkok 10110
telephone : +66.2.391 9919
facsimile : +66.2.391 9969
info@sareerarom.com
www.sareerarom.com

The Sarojin
60 Moo 2, Kukkak, Takupa,
Phang Nga
telephone : +66.76.427 900
facsimile : +66.76.427 906
info@sarojin.com
www.sarojin.com

Sheraton Krabi Beach Resort
155 Moo 2, Nong Thale,
Muang Krabi, Krabi 81000
telephone : +66.75.628 000
facsimile : +66.75.628 028
sheraton.krabi@sheraton.com
www.sheraton.com/krabi

Sila Evason Hideaway + Spa at Samui
9/10 Moo, Baan Plai Laem, Bophut,
Koh Samui, Surathani 84320
telephone : +66.77.245 678
facsimile : +66.77.245 671
reservations-samui@evasonhideaways.com
www.sixsenses.com/hideaway-samui

Siri Sathorn
27 Soi Saladaeng 1, Silom Road,
Silom, Bangrak, Bangkok 10500
telephone : +66.2.266 2345
facsimile : +66.2.267 5555
reservation@sirisathorn.com
www.sirisathorn.com

SriLanta
111 Moo 6 Klongnin Beach,
Koh Lanta Yai Krabi 81150
telephone : +66.75.697 288
facsimile : +66.75.697 289
srilanta@srilanta.com
www.srilanta.com

The Sukhothai Bangkok
13/3 South Sathorn Road,
Bangkok 10120
telephone : +66.23.448 888
facsimile : +66.23.448 899
info@sukhothai.com
www.sukhothai.com

Swissôtel Nai Lert Park Bangkok
2 Wireless Road, Bangkok 10330
telephone : +66.2.253 0123
facsimile : +66.2.254 8740
reservations@nailertpark.swissotel.com
www.nailertpark.swissotel.com

Trisara
60/1 Moo 6, Srisoonthorn Road,
Cherngtalay, Talang, Phuket
telephone : +66.76.310 100
facsimile : +66.76.310 300
email: reservations@trisara.com
www.trisara.com

Twinpalms Phuket
106/46 Moo 3, Surin Beach Road,
Cherng Talay, Phuket 83110
telephone : +66.76 316 500
facsimile : +66.76 316 599
book@twinpalms-phuket.com
www.twinpalms-phuket.com

Veranda Resort + Spa
737/12 Mung Talay Road Cha Am,
76120 Phetchaburi
telephone : +66.22.164 872/3 (office)
telephone : +66.32.709 000-99 (resort)
facsimile : +66.26.116 710
rsvn@verandaresortandspa.com
www.verandaresortandspa.com

Vertigo Grill + Moon Bar
Banyan Tree Bangkok,
21/100 Sathorn Road,
Bangkok 10120
telephone : +66.2.679 1200
facsimile : +66.2.679 1199
bangkok@banyantree.com
www.banyantree.com

Zeavola
11 Moo 8 Laem Tong, Koh Phi Phi,
Ao Nang, Krabi 81000
telephone : +66.75.627 000
facsimile: +66.75.627.025
info@zeavola.com
www.zeavola.com